SANDY LESBERG'S ONE HUNDRED
GREAT RESTAURANTS
OF AMERICA

SANDY LESBERG'S ONE HUNDRED
GREAT RESTAURANTS
OF AMERICA

A Personal Selection

Including 100 Specialty Recipes

CROWN PUBLISHERS, INC.   ONE PARK AVENUE   NEW YORK, N.Y. 10016

Design: Mareen Trenti
Illustrations: Judy Parenio
Graphic Production: Filmar Graphics, Inc., San Diego, CA

Inquiries should be addressed to Crown Publishers, Inc., One Park Avenue, New York, New York 10016

Printed in the United States of America

Published simultaneously in Canada by General Publishing Company Limited

Library of Congress Catalog Card Number 81-2286

ISBN: 0-517-539888

10 9 8 7 6 5 4 3 2 1

First edition

Contents

Contents

Introduction

The word "great" is a relative term and one that is often misused. When it appears in the title of this book it must be subject to particular scrutiny. Purists use only the criterion of a cuisine to evaluate a restaurant. Ultra purists limit themselves to the taste of the food. I am not quite so disciplined and tend therefore to be more liberal in my attitude toward the search for excellence. For me, the total experience has relevance. I am frequently asked, as are most people, "What's your favorite restaurant?" and I always say, "It depends on how I feel."

Classic French cuisine, when presented without tricks and without excessive pretention, is in many ways the most consistently satisfying food one can find. But of course there are many other dishes whose origins lie far afield from the French and are equally satisfying. Some restaurants have extraordinarily long menus with many house specialties and perhaps only a handful of menu items are done really well. But on the basis of those items, a restaurant can be seriously recommended. Other restaurants have short menus with a few outstanding items but also have inspiring ambiance or a fantastic view. For the most part, a combination of consistently fine food preparation of at least a half dozen chef's specialties together with some external feature such as an atmosphere that matches your mood will produce what might be recognized as a "great restaurant."

Here in America we are really blessed because all the important cuisines of the world have been brought here in true and honorable form so that we can be selective about where we eat and what we eat. More recently we're even learning "how" to eat. We all know that a fine meal is a full evening's activity and not merely something to be sandwiched in between a day's work and a night at the theatre.

The restaurants presented in this book at length, as well as those on the longer list at the back of the book, are all to be trusted and for that reason alone I bring them to your attention. I make no claim that every item on every menu will please your palate all the time or perhaps not even some of the time. But given the vagaries of your own mood and the proclaimed culinary inclination of the restaurant in question, I can assure you satisfaction at the very least, and a genuinely enlightening experience if both you and the chef come together at the right moment. So "great" is a relative term—and every restaurant in this book has at least a touch of greatness. Some offer much more than others. I leave it to you to discover the treasures among them.

Sandy Lesberg

Eastern Region

connecticut

district of columbia

maryland

massachusetts

new york

vermont

Griswold

Proprietor: William Winterer

Essex, Connecticut 06426
(203) 767-0991

The **Griswold Inn** has been providing New England-style food and lodging for more than 200 years. It is located in Essex, an attractive colonial village that boasts a number of carefully maintained houses of Revolutionary War vintage. This Inn is an outstanding example of the architecture and decor of the period.

A handsome white frame exterior sets the tone for a truly authentic early American interior. Drinks and musical entertainment are offered in the Tap Room. Originally a classroom, this part of the Griswold dates from 1738. It is dominated by an antique potbellied stove and a steamboat-Gothic bar.

There are several dining rooms including the Library, a book-lined room with a wood-burning fireplace; the original parlor of the Inn; the Steamboat Room, with appropriate decor ranging from binnacles to bells; the Gun Room, with its collection of 15th century firearms; and the Covered Bridge Room, constructed from an abandoned New Hampshire covered bridge. Integrated throughout the dining and drinking rooms of the Griswold Inn are displays of steamboat prints by Currier & Ives and other important lithographers, the Antonio Jacobsen Collection of Marine Oils, 55 rare antique handguns and rifles, and an extensive collection of various other artifacts from the riverboat era.

Authentic New England cuisine is as much a part of the Griswold Inn as its atmosphere. Entrées feature the Inn's own "1776 Brand" sausages made from original colonial recipes and served many different ways. There also are broiled New England lobster and home fried clams prepared fresh from the sea, as well as baked stuffed fillet of sole Newburg, broiled salmon with lemon butter, grilled shrimp oregano on long grain rice, and broiled king crab legs with drawn butter.

Among the meat and game bird dishes are New England fried chicken with biscuits and honey, Yankee pot roast of beef Jardinière, roast duckling with orange sauce, roast prime rib of beef with fresh horseradish, and Canadian quail in a nest of Bulgar wheat.

The Griswold Inn is open for lunch and dinner every day of the year, with the exception of Christmas Eve and Christmas Day. Reservations are suggested. There are no special dress requirements. American Express, Mastercharge, and Visa are honored. Prices are moderate to moderately expensive.

Inn

MUSSELS IN CREAM

4 cups (.95 liter) half and half

1/2 cup (120 milliliters) butter

1/2 cup (120 milliliters) flour

2 tablespoons (30 milliliters) Worcestershire sauce

1 tablespoon (15 milliliters) minced onion

1 garlic clove, minced, or 1/8 teaspoon (.6 milliliter) garlic powder

1/4 teaspoon (1.25 milliliters) salt

dash of white pepper

40 mussels, scrubbed and rinsed, beards removed

1 cup (240 milliliters) butter, cut into small pieces

1 cup (240 milliliters) dry white wine

2 tablespoons (30 milliliters) minced fresh parsley

To prepare the sauce: heat the cream in a 2-quart (1.9-liter) saucepan; do not boil. In a small saucepan, melt the 1/2 cup (120 milliliters) butter and stir in the flour with a whisk to make a roux. Cook over low heat, stirring constantly for 2-3 minutes; do not permit the roux to change color. Whisk the roux into the heated cream, then season with Worcestershire sauce, onion, garlic, salt, and pepper. Simmer 30 minutes, whisking occasionally, then strain and set aside.

Place the mussels into an 8-quart (7.6-liter) or larger heavy saucepan or kettle. Add the remaining butter and wine and heat until the butter is melted. Cover and simmer 3-5 minutes or until the mussels open. Discard any mussels that do not open. Add the cream sauce and parsley and serve the mussels immediately in a large tureen or in individual bowls with the sauce poured over.

Serves: 4-6

Wine: *Chardonnay*

Cantina d'Italia Ristorante is a cozy, unpretentious haven serving remarkably good northern Italian cuisine. The menu is based primarily on regional specialties of the Italian provinces of Piemonte, Val d'Aosta, and Liguria, with other areas of the Italian peninsula also represented.

The Cantina d'Italia wine list is exclusively Italian, with the majority of the selections coming from the Piemonte area.

The Antipasto di Verdura con salami is the traditional Italian appetite stimulator. It is prepared with roasted red, yellow, and green peppers combined with peas, cauliflower, broccoli, string beans, onions, tomatoes, sliced salami, and navy beans, served chilled in a portion sufficient for two. If you like seafood, another preparation for two is Savoiarda di Frutti di Mare—a fresh seafood antipasto with scallops, shrimp, topneck clams, mussels, and calamari, combined with a "giardiniera" of imported Italian pickled vegetables and seasoned with lemon juice and olive oil.

Unique among pasta specialties is the Tagliatelle Verde con le Cozze—freshly made green basil ribbon noodles in a sauce of fresh mussels, tomatoes, and garlic. Another fine pasta dish, Pappardelle al Modo Genovese, consists of broad noodles tossed with pesto, a classic Genovese sauce prepared with basil leaves, olive oil, garlic, pine nuts, and serdo cheese.

Something you may not have enjoyed before is Coniglio al Barolo—rabbit, first marinated in Barolo wine, then cooked with fresh vegetables, cloves, bitter chocolate, and Italian Mouquin brandy. Another first may be "Ran," a Piemonte specialty made from frogs' legs, prepared with garlic and cooked together with Arborio rice, seasoned with sage, nutmeg, cream, butter, Parmesan cheese, and a dash of Mouquin brandy. Another unusual dish, prepared specially to

Cantina d'Italia Ristorante

1214-A 18th Street, N.W.
Washington, D.C. 20036
(202) 659-1830

Proprietor/Chef:
Joseph Muran de Assereto

seal in juices and mingle flavors, is Trance di Branzino 'al Cartoccio con Rosmarino—fresh rockfish steak baked in parchment paper, with fresh rosemary, lemon juice, and butter.

Cantina d'Italia is open for lunch and dinner Monday through Friday. Reservations are recommended. There is no formal dress code. Major credit cards are accepted. Prices are moderate to expensive.

RISOTTO AL BAROLO

1 medium-sized yellow onion, finely chopped

4 tablespoons (60 milliliters) butter

1 1/2 cups (360 milliliters) Arborio rice

1 cup (240 milliliters) seasoned chicken broth

1 bottle Barolo wine

1 cup (240 milliliters) freshly grated Parmesan cheese

In a large frying pan, sauté the chopped onion in 3 tablespoons (45 milliliters) of butter over medium heat until golden. Add the rice and broth, stirring constantly with a wooden spoon so the rice does not burn. When all of the broth has been absorbed, add 3 cups (720 milliliters) of wine. Continue to stir until the rice is tender, approximately 20-25 minutes. (Note: as the rice cooks, it may require additional wine.) When cooked, the rice should be moist, not dry.

When ready to serve, stir in the remaining butter and the Parmesan cheese.

Serves: 4

Wine: *A dry red Gattinara from Piemonte*

Rive Gauche

3200 M Street, N.W.
Washington, D.C. 20007
(202) 333-6440

Rive Gauche has been serving gourmet meals for twenty-five years. When it first opened, there was no other restaurant for a half mile in any direction. Today, Rive Gauche is surrounded by eating places and its volume of business has not been significantly affected. This is a tribute to the consistency and excellence of its cuisine.

The opulent dining room suggests formality. On each white tablecloth is set a small bouquet of flowers, a pepper mill, crystal glassware, and silver place settings. There are gold on white drapes surrounding the windows and bronze sculptures centered in front of the daylight. Chandeliers hang over comfortable and elegant red-cushioned chairs.

You will be delighted to discover a number of authentic and delicious French preparations at Rive Gauche. Chef de Cuisine Michel Laudier prepares Soufflé de Homard Plaza-Athenée, Côte de Veau Sauté aux Morilles, Quenelles de Brochet Nantua, and others. Smoked ham with melon and Coquille de Crabe Véronique are fine cold and hot appetizers. Six soups—from Oignon Gratinée to Gaspacho Andalou—are specially prepared, as are the variety of salads and vegetables, including the Coeurs de Palmier Vinaigrette and Haricots Vert fins au Beurre.

Rive Gauche serves cocktails and offers an extensive selection of imported and domestic wines.

Lunch is served Monday through Saturday from 12:00 p.m.–2:30 p.m., dinner seven days a week from 6:00 p.m.–10:30 p.m. Reservations are recommended, dress is formal, and major credit cards are honored. Prices are expensive.

CÔTE DE VEAU SAUTÉ AUX MORILLES

4 8-ounce (224-gram) veal chops

salt and pepper, to taste

flour, as needed

2 ounces (60 milliliters) butter

2 teaspoons (10 milliliters) chopped shallots

2 ounces (56 grams) morels, or sliced white mushrooms

2 ounces (60 milliliters) Madeira wine

8 ounces (240 milliliters) heavy cream

4 ounces (120 milliliters) brown stock

Season the chops with salt and pepper and dust with flour. Cook them slowly in a sauté pan with butter, then place the chops on a serving tray. Discard the cooking fat. Add the shallots and mushrooms to the pan, sauté them for a few seconds, then add the Madeira wine. Cook for a few minutes. Add the cream and brown stock and cook for 5 minutes. Correct the seasoning, then pour the sauce over the veal and serve.

Serves: 4

Wine: *Beaujolais*

Sans Souci serves classical French cuisine in a comfortable, split-level dining room with 19th century decor. Impressionist paintings hang on wood paneled walls, and replicas of street gas lamps are strategically placed throughout the room. This is one of the most important restaurants in Washington, both politically and culinarily.

The food is uniformly superb. Sans Souci has often been called upon by the White House to provide late night take-out meals for members of the cabinet.

This restaurant offers Filets de Sole au Caviar and Canard aux Peches, two unusual entrées, while the traditional French selections are anything but ordinary. The Chateaubriand Grille Béarnaise Bouquetière and even the Truite Amandine have a unique aroma and taste. They are prepared by Chef Bernard Eloy who first worked at La Tour D'Argent in Paris. Proprietor Pierre Sosnitsky also trained in the French capitol.

Sans Souci's wine list has featured a wide variety of imported vintages for over fifteen years. For dessert, the Soufflé au Choix for two is a treat—a perfect way to complete your Sans Souci evening.

Sans Souci is open daily, except Sunday, for lunch from 12:00 p.m. to 2:00 p.m. and for dinner from 6:00 p.m. to 10:30 p.m. Dress is formal, reservations are required, and all major credit cards are honored. Prices are moderately expensive.

Sans Souci Restaurant

726 17th Street, N.W.
Washington, D.C. 20006
(202) 298-7424

Proprietor: Pierre Sosnitsky
Chef: Bernard Eloy

CHOUCROUTE DE POISSONS

4 pounds (1.8 kilograms) fresh sauerkraut

2 cloves

4 juniper berries

1 small bay leaf

1/4 teaspoon (1.25 milliliters) caraway seeds

4-5 sprigs parsley or 6 bruised peppercorns

2 tablespoons (30 milliliters) butter or oil

1 cup (240 milliliters) chopped onion

2 cups (480 milliliters) dry white wine

1/4 cup (60 milliliters) finely chopped shallots

2 cups (480 milliliters) heavy cream

salt and white pepper, to taste

1/2 pound (227 grams) smoked fish (haddock, chub, eel, or salmon)

milk, as needed

fish stock or clam juice, as needed

water, as needed

1 1/2-2 pounds (681-908 grams) of at least 2 kinds of fin fish: rockfish, sea bass, salmon, halibut, or angle fish

16-20 medium shrimp, shelled

8-10 sea scallops, cut in half

Wash the sauerkraut in warm water, squeeze out the liquid, and set to drain in a strainer. Prepare the bouquet garni by tying the cloves, juniper berries, bay leaf, caraway seeds, and parsley in cheesecloth.

Heat 1/2 the butter or oil in a Dutch oven or other heavy casserole. Add the onions and sauté until just soft. Add the sauerkraut, the wine, and the bouquet garni. Bring the mixture to a boil, cover the casserole, and lower the heat. Simmer approximately 1 hour for crisp sauerkraut or 2 hours for softer sauerkraut.

Heat the remaining butter or oil in a separate saucepan. Add the shallots and cook until softened. Add the cream and simmer for 10 minutes. Season to taste with salt and pepper.

Heat the smoked fish in a separate pan in milk.

Cover the bottom of a large sauté pan with half fish stock (or clam juice) and half water. Bring to a boil. Cut the fin and shell fish into serving pieces, add to the sauté pan, and cook 3-5 minutes or until fish is firm but not tough.

Arrange the fish atop the sauerkraut and spoon about 1/3 of the cream sauce over all. Serve the remaining sauce in a gravy boat.

Serves: 8-10

Chesapeake Restaurant

1701 North Charles Street
Baltimore, Maryland 21201
(301) 837-7711

Proprietor: Richard P. Friedman

One of the most highly honored eating establishments on the East Coast is the **Chesapeake Restaurant** in Baltimore. It was opened in 1904 by the Friedman family and has continued to be a family-run organization ever since. Today, the original family traditions of dining comfort and quality are safeguarded by the founder's grandson Richard Friedman, who, in addition to his restaurant family heritage, has also received formal training and practical experience in several other food service atmospheres.

The Chesapeake Restaurant's warm nautical theme creates a homey ambiance. Each of the several dining areas features a varying use of open brick work, wood paneling, and historic naval battle prints. The immaculately set tables are highlighted by the Chesapeake's exclusive maroon and white engraved china.

The menu emphasizes fresh, local seafood—all manner of shellfish, in particular. Jumbo Imperial crab is the popular house specialty. The list of beef, lamb, and duck dishes is as impressive as the seafood offerings—especially the prime rib and the popular Texas-style spareribs.

In addition to the fine selection of wines available, the Chesapeake Restaurant also offers a broad choice of imported and domestic beers, either on tap or in bottles. The dessert list isn't thin either. Its offerings include Mocha Ice Cream Cake, Black Forest Cake, and Chocolate Mousse Pie.

The Chesapeake Restaurant is open for lunch, Monday through Friday, and dinner seven nights a week. Seating is 110, so reservations are a must. Jackets and ties are the preferred dress, and all major credit cards are accepted. Prices are moderate.

CRAB CAKES

5 pounds (2.25 kilograms) crab meat

4 eggs

2 1/2 cups (600 milliliters) mayonnaise

1/3 cup (80 milliliters) dry mustard

3 tablespoons (45 milliliters) Lea & Perrins Worcestershire sauce

1 green pepper, chopped medium-fine

4 pieces pimento, chopped medium-fine

1/3 cup (80 milliliters) chopped parsley

2 quarts (1.9 liters) fresh bread crumbs

oil or butter, to fry

Combine all the ingredients except butter or oil and mix together lightly. Form into cakes and let sit for 1 hour. Deep-fat fry the cakes until a golden brown, then serve.

Serves: 4-6

Danny's brought its distinctive French and American haute cuisine to the city of crabs and beer about 20 years ago. Under the ownership and dedicated management of the Dickman family, it's gained a reputation for consistent quality and is particularly renowned for flamed specialties. The dining areas, highlighted by L'Escoffier Room, are decorated in a restrained yet elegant style. Crystal chandeliers, mellow wood paneling, fresh flowers and candles on tables, leather chairs, white napery, and gold-trimmed china characterize this beautiful setting.

Every dish is cooked to order using fresh ingredients and unique sauces and dressings. In fact, Danny's reports that all recipes used are original house recipes, including breads and baked goods which are made from scratch on the premises. Many dishes require tableside preparation with Danny Dickman or his son Stuart doing the honors.

Dinner at Danny's is an occasion, particularly when begun with Smoked Salmon flown in from Scotland. Steak Diane Flambé with wild rice or Steak Au Poivre, Flambé à l'Armagnac, with wild rice, are superb beef dishes. Fresh Dover Sole is flown in from England and prepared several ways. There are also live broiled or steamed Maine Lobster, Lobster Thermidor, and seafood specialties such as Jumbo Shrimps or Rockfish—both stuffed with crabmeat.

There is a separate menu just for desserts and brandies. There are Grand Marnier or chocolate soufflés for two. Flambé desserts include Bananas Danny, Baked Alaska, Cherries Jubilee, and Crepes Suzette. Pres-

Danny's

1201 North Charles Street
Baltimore, Maryland 21201
(301) 539-1393

Proprietor: Danny Dickman

ent too are pastries, parfaits, sundaes, and a number of special coffees: Cafe Diable, Cappuccino l'Amore, Irish Coffee, and Dutch Coffee (Vandermint and coffee with whipped cream).

Danny's serves lunch on weekdays and dinner Monday through Saturday. Reservations are required. Men must wear jackets, but ties are optional. Major credit cards are accepted. Prices are expensive.

BEATRICE SALAD

4 tablespoons (60 milliliters) olive oil

1 tablespoon (15 milliliters) red wine vinegar

1 tablespoon (15 milliliters) Dijon mustard

salt and freshly ground pepper, to taste

2 ounces (56 grams) watercress

2 ounces (56 grams) endive

2 ounces (56 grams) sliced fresh mushrooms

Mix the oil and vinegar together, then add the mustard, salt, and pepper. Add the salad greens and mushrooms and toss lightly.

Serves: 4

There are very few restaurants in America that enjoy the reputation of **Jimmy's Harborside Restaurant** in Boston. It began as a nine-stool cafeteria in 1924 and became The Harborside in 1955. For 25 years, Jimmy's has been serving seafood as only the finest New England restaurants can.

The huge establishment is long and comparatively narrow. The panes of glass on the restaurant's far side reveal a panorama of historic Boston harbor. The decor and service is unpretentious. Tables are draped in white cloth, chairs are padded red, the carpet is red and blue, game fish and nets adorn the walls. The glassware is not crystal, your plates are not made of delicate china. You go to Jimmy's to enjoy the best seafood in America not to be awed by the accoutrements. The broiled scrod is indescribably good; the original baked stuffed filet of sole is like none other you have ever tasted; and the range of fish, crustacea, and other seafood preparations is wide if not overwhelmingly original. At Jimmy's you quite simply dine on the most delicious, naturally flavored, aromatic seafood you've ever encountered.

There are also a complete bar service and a lengthly wine list which is reasonably priced. The atmosphere is convivial—a New England seafood house that seats over five hundred people could hardly be otherwise.

Jimmy Doulos has worked in every phase of the operation during his 26 years with the restaurant. He has established a tradition that all other New England seafood restaurants can, and do, admire.

Jimmy's Harborside Restaurant is open six days a week for lunch and dinner. Jackets are required in the evening, and all major credit cards are accepted. Prices are moderately expensive.

Jimmy's Harborside Restaurant

242 Northern Avenue
Boston, Massachusetts 02210
(617) 423-1000   Proprietor: James Doulos

BAKED STUFFED FILLET OF SOLE WITH LOBSTER NEWBURG SAUCE

2 slices bread, trimmed and diced

1 tablespoon (15 milliliters) cracker crumbs

6 ounces (180 milliliters) butter, approximately

2 ounces (60 milliliters) sherry wine

1 teaspoon (5 milliliters) grated Parmesan cheese

1/2 pound (227 grams) lobster meat, cut in small pieces

4 7-8-ounce (196-224-gram) slices of fillet of sole

1 cup (240 milliliters) milk

2 tablespoons (30 milliliters) flour

1 cup (240 milliliters) light cream

paprika, as needed

To prepare the stuffing: mix the diced bread with the cracker crumbs, 4 tablespoons (60 milliliters) melted butter, 1/2 the sherry, Parmesan cheese, and 1/2 the lobster meat.

To prepare the fillets of sole: roll the sole with the stuffing, place them in a pan, brush lightly with butter, and add 1/2 the milk to keep them moist. Place in a 350° oven and bake for 10 minutes.

To prepare white sauce: place 4 tablespoons (60 milliliters) of melted butter in a saucepan, add the flour, and whip slowly. Add the remaining milk and cream, and simmer until thickened.

To prepare Lobster Newburg Sauce: Place 1 tablespoon (15 milliliters) butter in a saucepan, add the remainder of the lobster, sherry, and paprika, and sauté for 30 seconds. Add the white sauce and simmer for 5 minutes.

Pour the Newburg Sauce over the fillets and bake for 5 minutes at 350°, then serve.

Serves: 4

Wine: *Dry white Chablis or Burgundy*

Locke-Ober

General Manager: Frank A. Curro

3 & 4 Winter Place
Boston, Massachusetts
(617) 542-1340

The **Locke-Ober Café** boasts a reputation for fine food that has attracted visitors from every part of the world. The buildings in which it is located were constructed before the city's Building Department began keeping construction records. It is known that by 1859, a cellar cafe was being operated in the alley off the Common leading from Winter Street into Temple Place. By 1875, the Café proper was already doing business on the very spot in which it stands today.

Maintained in their near-original condition are the L-shaped mahogony bar, a bronze statue (now used principally as a hat rack), polished metal steam dishes, a Kruse Check cash register, a system of weights and counterweights used to lift the covers which adorn the bar (these were designed in Germany by Reed and Barton silversmiths), an Italian oil painting, and other items large and small, too numerous to list here.

Locke-Ober is a New England landmark, a piece of Americana with a loyal following.

More than tradition contributes to that kind of standing. The food and service are exemplary. A sampling of Locke-Ober's specialties includes Anchovies, Winter Place; Baked Oysters, Winter Place; Baked Clams, Casino; Clear Green Turtle Soup au Sherry; Baked Lobster Savannah; Filet Mignon of Beef, Mirabeau; Breast of Chicken (under glass), Richmond; Sweetbreads (under glass), Eugene; Sultana Roll, Claret Sauce; English Trifle. A wide selection of imported and domestic wines is also available.

General Manager Frank A. Curro has been at Locke-Ober for 37 years—first as a busboy, then as a waiter, then as maitre d'. Today, he directs the entire staff.

The Café is open for lunch and dinner six days a week, not on Sundays or holidays. Reservations are recommended, all major credit cards are honored, and jackets and ties are required in the evening. Prices are moderately expensive.

Café

BAKED LOBSTER SAVANNAH

2 ounces (60 milliliters) butter

2 cups (480 milliliters) sliced mushrooms

1 cup (240 milliliters) diced green pepper

1 generous tablespoon (15 milliliters) Spanish paprika

1 1/2 cups (360 milliliters) sherry wine

salt and pepper, to taste

4 cups (.95 liter) cream sauce, prepared

1/2 cup (120 milliliters) diced pimentos

4 3-pound (1.35-kilogram) lobsters, boiled and cooled

grated Parmesan cheese, as needed

To prepare the sauce: heat the butter to the melting point in a large saucepan, then add the mushrooms and green pepper. Cook until tender. Add paprika and stir in the sherry and cook until the liquid is reduced by half. Salt and pepper to taste, add cream sauce and pimentos, and blend well. Bring to a simmer.

While vegetables are cooking, remove claws and knuckles from the lobsters. Hold each lobster with its top side up. With kitchen shears, cut an oval opening in top of shell from tip of tail to base of head. Remove meat from the body, claws, and knuckles. Cut in large dice after discarding the intestinal vein and stomach.

Add the diced lobster meat to the sauce and simmer slowly for 10 minutes. Divide the mixture evenly and spoon back into the lobster shells. Dust with grated cheese and brown in a 375° oven for 15 minutes, then serve.

Serves: 4

Wine: *Pinot Chardonnay*

Maison Robert

45 School Street
Boston, Massachusetts 02108
(617) 244-2395

Maison Robert's elegant French cuisine can be enjoyed in Boston's old 'City Hall'—a New England landmark constructed in 1865. The building has recently been restored to its original classic beauty. The restaurant has been owned and operated by Lucien Robert for nine years.

A unique feature of Maison Robert is its division into two restaurants. The elegant *Bonhomme Richard* is on the upper floor and has French Second Empire styling. Magnificent crystal chandeliers, high ceilings, mirrors, and potted palms all contribute to the gracious setting in which lunch and dinner are served six days a week. In contrast to the elaborate second floor setting, *Ben's Cafe*, on ground level, has a warm, simple contemporary oak interior which houses four dining rooms and a lounge-bar. Here, you can dine on the outdoor terrace overlooking a manicured lawn and a statue of Benjamin Franklin. Each restaurant has its own kitchen, gourmet menu, and wine list. The common wine cellar is especially known for its Burgandies and Bordeaux vintages.

M. Robert was born in Normandy and trained at Pruniers in Paris. He is one of the burgeoning breed of classically trained Master Chef owners whose life's dedication is to create and prepare the finest French foods. He and his wife, Ann, whom he met after her graduation from Radcliffe College, are committed to maintaining the highest standard of service and cuisine. They personally oversee virtually every aspect of their restaurant's operation.

No one dish is the 'specialty of the house' at Maison Robert, but both restaurants are known for their Mousse of Pike, Lobster with Whiskey Sauce, Rack and Saddle of Lamb, and Roast Chicken with cream.

Bonhomme Richard is open for lunch and dinner weekdays and Saturdays; *Ben's Cafe* is open seven days. Jackets and ties are recommended, and major credit cards are welcome. Prices are moderately expensive upstairs and modest downstairs.

ESTOUFFADE DE LOTTE AU MUSCADET
(Monkfish in Muscadet Wine)

2 finely chopped shallots

   butter, as needed

1 sliced white of leek

1 finely diced carrot

1 1/2 pounds (681 grams) fresh monkfish cut into 1 inch (2.5 centimeter) squares

2 cups (480 milliliters) Muscadet wine

6 ounces (180 milliliters) whipping cream

   skinless white grapes, to garnish (optional)

Pan fry the shallots in butter, then add the leek whites and stir well. Add the chopped carrot and continue to pan fry. Add the fish, toss and mix thoroughly while cooking. Add the wine and bring almost to a boil. Cover, remove from heat, and allow to sit for 5-7 minutes.

With a slotted spoon, remove the fish and vegetables from the liquid. Return the liquid to heat and reduce to a glaze. When thick and bubbly, remove from heat. Add a piece of butter and the whipping cream. Return to slow heat, but be careful not to allow the mixture to boil.

(If desired, add the grapes to the fish and vegetable mixture.) Place the fish and vegetable mixture on a heated serving dish and cover with the sauce. Serve.

Serves: 4-6

Wine: *Muscadet*

Gage & Tollner

Proprietors: Edward S. Dewey and
John B. Simmons

372 Fulton Street
Brooklyn, New York
(212) 875-5181

With few exceptions, **Gage & Tollner** appears exactly the way it did in 1889 when Messrs. Gage and Tollner opened the restaurant in its present location, but the restaurant's roots were actually established ten years earlier down the street by Charles Gage. In 1884, Eugene Tollner joined Charles in building his little restaurant into one of the most renowned in all of New York City. In 1889, they moved to larger, permanent quarters at their present address. Both men continued to be active in the business until 1911. Since then, owners have come and gone, but the integrity of Gage & Tollner's original concept has always remained intact.

Today, Gage & Tollner is presided over by Ed Dewey and John Simmons; their combined years of experience ensure that the food in this famous turn-of-the-century American restaurant will continue to be fresh fish, seafood, steaks and chops served at

their best in a congenial atmosphere that has stopped time.

Incidentally, the building, both inside and out, has been officially designated an historical landmark. Each evening, the original gas chandeliers are lit, casting a haunting glow on the tall mirrors, velvet panels, mahogany tables, and cherry woodwork.

The menu is broad and encompasses the finest traditional American cuisine: seafood cocktails and soups, lobster, crabmeat, clam and oyster specialties, fresh fish, chicken, beef, lamb, and mutton dishes. They're prepared in a variety of ways and served by a corps of experienced waiters; some of them have been with the establishment over 30 years. A large selection of American and imported wines is available.

Gage & Tollner is open seven days a week. Be sure to call for a reservation. Major credit cards are accepted. Prices are moderate.

BAY SCALLOPS NEWBURG

2 tablespoons (30 milliliters) butter

2 tablespoons (30 milliliters) flour

paprika, to color

pinch of salt

2 cups (480 milliliters) warm milk

2 ounces (60 milliliters) sherry

1 cup (240 milliliters) raw scallops

toast points

In a heavy saucepan, melt the butter. Add the flour to the melted butter, stir, then cook together for 2 minutes to make a roux.

To prepare the sauce: add paprika to the roux until the desired color is reached, then add a pinch of salt. Gradually stir in the warm milk and cook, stirring constantly with a wooden spoon or a wire whisk until the sauce reaches a thick but smooth consistency. Add the sherry to the sauce.

Add the scallops and cook them gently in the sauce for 1-2 minutes.

Serve on toast points.

Serves: 2-3

Café

Café des Artistes has become one of those places everyone wants to be seen in, where influential people, the tastemakers of the country, congregate. There is something about this place that draws them—something beyond the solid, dependable food that is prepared and served so well. There is an air of warmth, hospitality, and intellectual ferment that is conducive to good talk and the exchange of ideas. This ambiance has had ample time to develop; the restaurant opened in 1917.

The most famous, easily noticed, and remembered features of the decor are the $1 million collection of large murals of nudes frolicking in bucolic settings, done by the noted American painter Howard Chandler Christy.

The distinctive ambiance is further enhanced by mirrored walls, soft antique lights, fresh flowers, and displays of fresh fruits. New in the bar room are exhibits of paintings by celebrities. Also shown are original sketches for the stage sets of the Metropolitan Opera, New York State Theater, New York City Center Opera and Ballet.

Appetizers by Chef Andre Guillou are imaginative. His special creations include: a good, pink Gravlak Salmon marinated with dill; Sautéed Snails with garlic, onions and Prosciutto; and Fresh Rel, marinated in wine and lemon. Soup offerings include chilled Seafood Gazpacho, a cold curried Cream of Cucumber, and a hot Cream of Leeks & Potato Soup.

A special entrée is the Bourride with Aioli, a fish casserole Provençale style. Originated in the region around Marseilles, the Bourride is made with assorted fish, orange peel, saffron, tomato, garlic, onion, and olive oil. It is served with aioli sauce over slices of dry bread. Another unusual dish is the Silver Hill Quail, Braised with Juniper Berry Butter. The Entrecôte with Shallots and Mushrooms; Fettuccini with Bacon, Sausages and

des Artistes

One West 67th Street
New York, New York 10023
(212) TR 7-3500

Proprietor: George Lang

Broccoli; a generous portion of Gigot d'Agneau (roast leg of lamb served with flageolets); and the tender, flavorful Sautéed Calf's Liver with Avocado are also delicious.

Café des Artistes is open every day for lunch and dinner. Saturday and Sunday brunch, served along with the International Herald Tribune and many out-of-town newspapers, have become neighborhood traditions. You must call for a reservation in this 100-seat restaurant, particularly for weekend dining. Informal attire is in style here. All major credit cards are accepted. Prices are moderate to moderately expensive.

GARLIC SNAILS WITH PROSCIUTTO

1 1/2 cups (360 milliliters) chopped onion

1/2 cup (120 milliliters) shallots

4 tablespoons (60 milliliters) butter

1 teaspoon (5 milliliters) chopped garlic

10 thin slices Prosciutto ham, julienne

6 7 1/2-ounce (1.26-kilogram) cans of snails (12 dozen), drained

salt and freshly ground pepper, to taste

chopped parsley and tarragon, to garnish

Soften the onions and shallots in butter, but do not allow them to brown. Add the garlic and cook, stirring for 1 minute. Stir in the Prosciutto and then the snails. Cook, stirring to blend the flavors. Season with salt and pepper. Serve as a hot appetizer in a puff pastry shell or on rye toast, garnished with chopped parsley and tarragon.

Serves: 10 or more

"I am a host and I want my guests to have a sense of occasion when they come here," says **La Caravelle**'s co-owner Roger Fessaguet. He had been executive chef at this great restaurant for 20 years and only recently handed those reins to André Moisan. Fessaguet established the classic haute cuisine of La Caravelle and now, with Robert Meyzen, oversees the formal elegance of cuisine and service.

La Caravelle is a place where you can enjoy luxury eating in classic European style, seated on plush scarlet banquettes. Each morning an hors d'oeuvre trolley is set up with pâtés and terrines, smoked salmon, vegetables, and meats in aspic. No music is piped in, so there is a minimum of distraction at the well-appointed tables. The dining room is cozy with a relatively low ceiling. Whites and light reds predominate, and there are easy-on-the-eye murals of Parisian scenes painted by artist Jean Pages. The waiters in black tie are friendly, formal, and efficient. The rose on your table is florist-fresh.

Some popular entrées are fresh turbot (flown in from France), veal with a mustard-tarragon cream sauce, Quenelles de Brochets Homardine, and the roast of the day which is sliced at your table. The wine list is virtually all French, as are the desserts. The cakes, soufflés, pastries, and mousses are prepared on the premises. These creations are all examples of culinary artistry. La Caravelle emphasizes the best of classic haute cuisine and is really one of the great dining establishments of the world.

La Caravelle is open six days a week for lunch and dinner. Reservations should be made well in advance. Formal dress is required. All major credit cards are accepted. Prices are moderately expensive to expensive.

Caravelle

33 West 55th Street
New York, New York 10019
(212) 586-4252

Proprietors:
Roger Fessaguet and Robert Meyzen
Chef: André Moisan

BASS POCHÉ AUX HUÎTRES

salt and pepper, to taste

2 bay leaves

pinch of thyme

2 garlic cloves

1 striped bass, enough to serve 8-10 people

court-bouillon, enough to cover

fresh parsley and decorated lemon halves, to garnish

48-60 oysters

pinch of chopped shallots

1/4 quart (240 milliliters) white wine

1/2 quart (480 milliliters) fumet of sole

pinch of chopped shallots

pinch of chopped mushroom tails

butter, to sauté

1 quart (950 milliliters) heavy cream

1/2 quart (480 milliliters) fish velouté

juice of 1 lemon

parcels of butter, as needed

To prepare the bass: add salt, pepper, bay leaves, thyme, and garlic cloves to the inside of the bass. Tie up and wrap in a napkin; tie up again. Poach in court-bouillon for 20 minutes. Let cool off in liquid. Remove fish from liquid; do not skin. Dress on napkin with fresh parsley and decorated lemon halves.

To prepare the oysters: poach the oysters in pinch of chopped shallots, white wine, and fumet of sole, then remove them. Cover oysters with a damp towel; reserve broth.

To prepare oyster sauce: simmer remaining shallots and mushroom tails in butter, then add oyster broth. Reduce until almost dry, then add cream. Reduce to sauce consistency, then add velouté. Cook for 1/2 hour. Pass mixture through a sieve, then season to taste. Finish with lemon juice and parcels of butter, then oysters.

Serve bass with oyster sauce on the side.

Serves: 8-10

Le Cirque is undoubtedly one of the finest restaurants in the United States. Each item on the menu is a delicacy. The proprietor, Sirio Maccioni, maintains a decorous good humor and a standard of excellence suitable for his top grade clientele. The decor is bright and cheery, and even though the food preparation and service is serious, the general atmosphere is relaxed.

Chef Alain Sailhac trained in France. His influence is felt at Le Cirque on both the lunch and dinner menus. The luncheon menu offers a $17.50 prix fixe three-course meal of unusual variety. You may choose from appetizers such as Pâté Laurencie and Crêpe Le Cirque. There are more than 15 entrées in the prix fixe offerings alone, including Suprême de Flounder Grillé-Dijonnaise; Quenelle de Brochet, Sauce Champagne; and Aiguillette de Caneton au Poivre Rose. For dessert there are patisseries, Crème Caramel, Mousse Opéra, and others.

If lunch is special, dinner is gala. There are literally dozens of superb appetizers and soups. A special fish selection is Fricassée de Lotte au Saffron; for beef, the Côte de Boeuf au Romarin Pour Deux is recommended. Vegetables are not mere appendages to entrées at Le Cirque; here they add an important dimension to your meal.

You can have a demi or carafe of wine or select a bottle from the imported and domestic vintages on their extensive list. You can also trust the house blanc or rouge.

Le Cirque is open for lunch and dinner six days a week. Jackets and ties are required, reservations are essential, and all major credit cards are honored. Prices are expensive.

Le Cirque

58 East 65th Street
New York, New York 10021
(212) 794-9292

Proprietor: Sirio Maccioni
Chef: Alain Sailhac

MILLE FEUILLES DE RIS DE VEAU AU CALVADOS

3 pounds (1362 grams) sweetbread

water, as needed

salt and pepper, to taste, as needed

1 bouquet garni

1 clove garlic

1 carrot, diced

1 small onion, diced

1 1/2 pounds (681 grams) mushrooms, escaloped

11 ounces (308 grams) butter

3 ounces (90 milliliters) Calvados

4 ounces (120 milliliters) flour

2 shallots, chopped

1/2 quart (480 milliliters) chicken stock

1/2 quart (480 milliliters) heavy cream

1 pound (454 grams) puff pastry dough

1/2 ounce (15 milliliters) meat glaze

Soak the sweetbread in water for 6 hours, then boil for 7 minutes while adding salt, pepper, bouquet garni, garlic, carrot, and onion. Remove from heat and let cool in its pan. Place sweetbread between two sheet pans and refrigerate overnight, pressed with a heavy weight. The next day, trim the sweetbread, then slice it 1/2 inch (1.3 centimers) thick.

In a separate saucepan, sauté the mushrooms with 3 ounces (84 grams) butter, salt, and pepper. Set aside. In the same butter, sauté the sweetbread until golden on both sides, then glaze with 2 ounces (60 milliliters) of Calvados and set aside.

Prepare roux by mixing flour into 4 ounces (112 grams) melted butter and cook over low heat for 10 minutes.

In a separate pan, sauté the chopped shallots with 2 ounces (56 grams) butter slowly for 5 minutes and add the remaining Calvados. Heat for 30 seconds, then add chicken stock and reduce for 10 minutes. Add heavy cream and reduce for 10 more minutes. Pour the reduction into the roux and whip for 3 minutes, then cook for 10 minutes while adding salt and pepper. Transfer the mixture to a pot and stir slowly while adding the remaining butter.

Form the pastry dough into 3 round sheets, each 1/8 inch (.3 centimeter) thick and 10 inches (25 centimeters) in diameter. Dock the pastry. Chill for 1 hour, then bake for 12 minutes in a 380° oven.

Place 2/3 of the sauce in a pan and slowly add the sweetbread and mushrooms.

Place one sheet of baked puff pastry in a genoise form of 8 inches (20 centimeters) and cover with one layer of sweetbread and mushrooms. Place a second sheet of pastry on top and cover with a second layer of sweetbread and mushrooms. Cover with the third sheet of pastry. Gently press down and transfer the mille feuilles to a plate, then remove the genoise form. Completely cover the mille feuilles with the remaining sauce.

Make a swirling design with meat glaze in a pastry bag, starting from the center. Serve very hot.

Serves: 8

Le Coup de Fusil

Proprietor: Marina de Brantes
Chef: Etienne Lizzi

160 East 64th Street
New York, New York 10021
(212) 751-9110

Le Coup de Fusil is a charming bit of France in New York, with food preparation firmly representing *nouvelle cuisine*. The energetic, demanding owner of this elegant establishment is Countess Marina de Brantes who is the sister-in-law of the President of France. The Countess is known for her inexhaustible zeal in exploring the culinary world and for perfecting new dishes which appear on the menu at frequent intervals. The menu, in fact, changes almost entirely every six weeks.

Le Coup de Fusil is plush and intimate with deep red and mirrored walls, an art-deco tin ceiling, etched glass panels dividing the room, wall lights with rose-shaped bulbs, engravings and old menus on the walls, flower sconces, soft banquettes, and small tables dressed in starched pink linen bearing candles and lovely fresh flowers.

The food is superb and is prepared with a delicacy that is the perfect expression of what the much-discussed *nouvelle cuisine* is all about. Seafood specialities include Saumoneau au Coulis de Cresson (baby salmon in a light cresson sauce), Filet de Lotte à la Julienne de Poireaux (a tasty angler fish with shredded leak), Filet de Lotte à la Nage (angler fish again, this time with a light vermouth sauce), and Rouget au Coulis de Tomate (red snapper with fresh tomato sauce).

Examples of fine aged beef entrées are the Entrecôte au Poivre Vert (shell steak with green peppercorns) and the Paillard de Boeuf Grille (a thin grilled shell steak). Two favorite creations are the Petit Poulet aux Trois Moutardes (chicken with a three-mustard sauce) and the Carre d'Agneau au Romarin (pink, tender lamb seasoned with rosemary).

For dessert, there is an extraordinary Fine Tarte Chaude aux Pommes Acidulées (a warm apple tart with a parchment-like crust topped with a layer of sweetened apples), Sorbet au Boysenberry, Mousse au Chocolat, Soufflé Glace, and Galette au Citron et Coulis de Fraises.

Le Coup de Fusil serves luncheon Monday through Friday, and dinner Monday through Saturday. Reservations are necessary. Gentlemen are expected to wear jackets and ties. All major credit cards are honored. Prices are expensive.

SAUMONEAU AU CRESSON

2 cups (480 milliliters) vermouth

2 tablespoons (30 milliliters) shallots, chopped

2 tablespoons (30 milliliters) fish stock

4 cups (.95 liter) heavy cream

salt and pepper, to taste

1/2 bunch of watercress, chopped

1 pound (454 grams) scallops

4-6 8-10-ounce (224-280-gram) baby salmons, boneless and headless

2 cups (480 milliliters) white wine

To prepare the sauce: reduce the vermouth and shallots in a saucepan until dry. Add the fish stock and 1/2 the heavy cream. Reduce until the consistency of thin custard. Add salt and pepper to taste and strain. Add chopped watercress at the last minute.

To prepare mousse: blend the scallops, the remaining heavy cream, salt, and pepper together in a food processor.

Stuff each salmon with mousse. Place the fish in the white wine in a foil-covered pan and poach in a 400° oven for 10 minutes.

Remove the skin on both sides of the salmon and serve with the sauce.

Serves: 4-6

Dining at **The Four Seasons** is much more than simply going out for dinner. It is an experience, both gastronomical and environmental. To begin with, it is luxury—open spaces, a pool of water, dramatic windows— a visual spectacle in celebration of the four seasons of the year. And every three months the decor is dramatically revised to welcome in the new season. This is true for some aspects of the menu as well, which brings me to a very important point.

The Four Seasons restaurant, first and foremost, prepares and serves superb food. The appetizers encompass everything from the finest imported caviar and ramekins of sweetbreads to salmon pâté and a galantine of capon. Entrées include the best broiled American steaks and chops to more exotic dishes like Grilled Entrecôte with Mustard Butter and Filet of Striped Bass in Phyllo Leaves. A wide assortment of international wines is available in all price ranges. California vineyards are especially well represented. Proceed with caution toward the Bourbon Mousse for dessert. Share it if you can; it's sinful.

The Four Seasons is one of the most interesting restaurants in New York City and should not be missed when visiting Manhattan. It is located in the midtown area and is open for lunch, cocktails, and dinner Monday through Saturday. Jackets are required, but ties are optional. Reservations are a must, and all major credit cards are welcomed. Prices are expensive.

Four Seasons

99 East 52nd Street
New York, New York 10022
(212) 754-9494

Proprietors:
Paul Kovi and Tom Margittai
Chef: Joseph (Seppi) Renggli

DUCKLING LIVER WRAPPED IN SPINACH

12 duckling livers

4 teaspoons (20 milliliters) canned green peppercorns with liquid

6 tablespoons (90 milliliters) brandy

1/3 cup (80 milliliters) Madeira wine

2 pounds (908 grams) large spinach leaves, blanched

1/2 pound (227 grams) butter

1/2 cup (120 milliliters) parsley, minced

1/2 teaspoon (2.5 milliliters) salt

juice of 1/2 lemon

2 egg yolks

6 hearts of palm, canned, quartered lengthwise

18 cherry tomatoes

18 black olives

18 boiled onions

24 melon balls

Separate each liver into 2 lobes and cut out the connective tubing. Make 2-3 holes in each lobe with the tip of a knife and place a green peppercorn in each hole. (There should be about 1 tablespoon or 15 milliliters of peppercorns left.) Pour 5 tablespoons (75 milliliters) of the brandy, all the Madeira, and about 1 tablespoon (15 milliliters) of the liquid from the can of peppercorns over the livers and set aside to marinate.

Reserve 24 very large, unbroken spinach leaves (or 48 smaller ones) for wrapping the livers and mince the rest. Mince the remaining green peppercorns with a bit of their liquid, then mash with the side of a knife to make a paste. Cream the butter with the minced spinach, parsley, mashed peppercorns, and salt. Beat in the lemon juice and the remaining brandy. Beat in the egg yolks, one at a time.

Center a heaping teaspoon (15 milliliters) of the flavored butter on one large spinach leaf (or on several smaller overlapping ones), place 1 piece of liver on top, and fold the spinach over to enclose the liver completely. Place seam side down in a large, buttered gratin dish. Repeat with the remaining spinach, butter, and liver.

Lay a strip of the heart of palm between each spinach package and pour the marinade from the livers over all. Cover and bake in a preheated 350° oven for 10 minutes, then add the tomatoes, olives, onions, and melon balls to garnish. Bake another 5 minutes, then serve.

Serves: 6

Restaurant Romeo

Proprietor: Salvatore Salta

30 West 56th Street
New York, New York 10019
(212) 246-5772

Restaurant Romeo Salta has been serving first class Italian cuisine for 25 years. The unceasing efforts of the Salta family have established a reputation that places them among the top of their field.

The menu presents a panorama of the best Italian recipes in all categories. The most distinguished wines of Italy are noted on a wine list printed on parchment paper.

Scampi alla Griglia Romeo (broiled giant shrimps), Combinazione Scampi e Vongole (broiled shrimps and clams), Salmone (smoked salmon), Pâté di Fegato (liver pâté), Carciofini all'Olio (hearts of artichokes in olive oil), and Antipasti Variati (an assortment of hors d'oeuvres) are superb appetizers.

The Romeo Salta soups are better than homemade. Zuppa all'Ortolano (Italian vegetable soup); Zuppa alla Panese (croutons, poached egg, and Parmesan cheese), Stracciatella (spinach, eggs, and Parmesan cheese), and Zuppa Zingarella (spinach and clams)—all are smooth and delicious.

Among some three dozen pasta dishes is an old Salta family recipe—Paglia e Fieno Papalina (white and green noodles with peas and Prosciutto). Other marvelous pasta dishes are Fettuccini Romeo (noodles with butter and cheese), Spaghettini alla Carbonara (noodles with bacon, eggs, fresh pepper, and cheese), Cannelloni Anna Maria Sabatini (large meat-stuffed macaroni), Spaghettini Aglio e Olio (noodles with olive oil, garlic, and parsley).

Seafood at Romeo Salta strikes just the right balance of fish and delicately spiced flavors. Some of the best dishes are Smoked Sturgeon with Fried Eggs; Calamari in Cassuola (squids in spiced tomato broth); and Scampi e Cappesante alle Mandorle (shrimps and scallops Amandine).

And of course, there are veal and chicken. Scaloppine Florio (veal, Marsala wine, and mushrooms); Spezzato de Pollo Romeo (chicken in small pieces, white wine, and chives); Scarpariello (chicken in small pieces with fresh chicken livers sautéed in olive oil,

Salta

with parsley and garlic) are all light, satisfying entrées. If you're in the mood for beef, try the Cuori di Filetto Remo (split filet mignon with rosemary and brandy sauce); it's cooked by your table.

Romeo Salta serves lunch and dinner Monday through Saturday. Call ahead for reservations at this very busy restaurant. Jackets for men are required. All major credit cards are honored. Prices are expensive.

SPAGHETTINI SPAMPINATO

32 ounces (960 milliliters) tomato sauce

8 ounces (240 milliliters) pesto, not oily

8 teaspoons (40 milliliters) crushed garlic

8 teaspoons (40 milliliters) softened butter

12 ounces (336 grams) spaghettini, cooked al dente

8 teaspoons (40 milliliters) Parmesan cheese

dash of freshly ground black pepper

In a pan, mix the tomato sauce, pesto, garlic, and butter together. Cook the mixture over low heat for 3-4 minutes. Discard any excess fat with a spoon. Add the spaghettini to the sauce, mix, and let cook for 1/2 minute longer. Add the cheese, freshly ground pepper, mix well, and serve.

Serves: 4

Wine: *Rosso Conero*

The Russian Tea Room is crowds, color, authentic Russian decor, gleaming samovars, year-round Christmas decorations, and celebrities dining elbow-to-elbow with ordinary folk. Located slightly to the east of Carnegie Hall, it is a gathering place for many people of note in the arts.

Waiters in colorful Russian tunics serve delicious classic Russian food. Their wine collection includes fine representatives of the products of California, France, Italy, Germany, and Spain.

Almost everyone starts with hot or cold borscht, those delicious hearty Russian soups served with flaky, meat-filled pirojoks. There are several types of caviar to suit your taste and pocketbook. Kholodetz is a melange of jellied meats, including chicken, beef, and veal. Then there are pickled herring, smoked salmon, and RTR Zakuska (Russian-style hors d'oeuvres) offering a bit of everything.

The blinchiki crepes are filled with cottage cheese, served with sour cream and red caviar; the nalistniki are filled with pâté and mushrooms.

Selections of main courses include their popular chicken specialty, Cotelette à la Kiev, marinated and skewered lamb Karsky Shaslik, Beef à la Stroganoff made the real Russian way, Half Roast Duckling Vereniki, and Kulebiaka—an unusual delicacy composed of pastry-wrapped layers of salmon or chicken and mushrooms.

The Russian Tea Room is open daily for lunch, dinner, and supper. Reservations are recommended. Gentlemen should wear jackets. All major credit cards are accepted. Prices are moderate to expensive.

Russian Tea Room

150 West 57th Street
New York, New York 10019
(212) 265-0947

Proprietor: Faith Stewart-Gordon
Chefs: Sixto Gonzalez and Tioshi Horita

HOT BORSCHT

3/4 cup (180 milliliters) finely chopped carrots

1 1/2 cups (360 milliliters) finely chopped onions

1 1/2 cups (360 milliliters) finely chopped beets

1 1/2 cups (360 milliliters) finely chopped celery

1 1/2 cups (360 milliliters) finely chopped parsnips

boiling water, as needed

2 tablespoons (30 milliliters) butter

3 cups (720 milliliters) beef stock

1 1/2 cups (360 milliliters) finely shredded cabbage

1 1/2 cups (360 milliliters) tomato pulp or stewed and strained tomatoes

salt and pepper, to taste

8 tablespoons (120 milliliters) thick sour cream at room temperature

finely chopped dill, as needed

Barely cover the carrots, onions, beets, celery, and parsnips with boiling water and boil gently, covered, for 20 minutes. Add butter, stock, cabbage, tomato pulp, salt, and pepper to the vegetables and boil for another 15 minutes. Place the soup in bowls and add 1 tablespoon (15 milliliters) sour cream to each. Sprinkle chopped dill on top and serve.

Serves: 8

Wine: *Pouilly Fumé or Chardonnay*

Sardi's overlooks Shubert Alley in the heart of New York's theater district and is considered *the* restaurant of the American theater. It is a "clubhouse" for actors, a home away from home for the stars and casts of every show on Broadway. The tradition of an opening-night party at Sardi's is long-established. So many celebrities dine there that their presence is no special event—it's expected.

The 59-year-old landmark restaurant reflects the warm, comfortable atmosphere developed during three generations of Sardi family ownership and management. The ambiance is much like that of an English club, and in spite of the name, Sardi's has never been a strictly Italian restaurant. It is known not only for the fun of celebrity watching, the network radio show "Luncheon at Sardi's," and the consistent quality of its continental cuisine, but also for some 1,200 caricatures of famous Sardi guests that line the walls.

One of the most popular of the entrée specialties has always been the Cannelloni au Gratin with Sardi Sauce. Other entrées include Lumb Crabmeat à la Sardi with asparagus tips and duchesse potatoes, Roast Prime Ribs of Beef Au Jus with baked potato and salad, Shrimp, Crabmeat, and Deep Sea Scallops Marinara with rice and peas.

Popular desserts are Boccone Dolce, Frozen Cake with Zabaglione sauce, Baked Alaska for two, and Fresh Strawberries with sour or sweet cream.

Sardi's serves luncheon and dinner daily, and brunch on Sunday. Reservations are necessary. Jackets and ties for men are preferred, but not required. All major credit cards are accepted. Prices are moderate to expensive.

Sardi's

234 West 44th Street
New York, New York 10036
(212) 221-8440

Proprietor: Vincent Sardi

BOCCONE DOLCE

4 egg whites

pinch of salt

1/4 teaspoon (1.25 milliliters) cream of tartar

1 1/3 cups (320 milliliters) sugar

6 ounces (168 grams) semisweet chocolate pieces

3 tablespoons (45 milliliters) water

3 cups (720 milliliters) cream

1 pint (470 milliliters) fresh strawberries, sliced

whole ripe strawberries to decorate (optional)

To prepare meringue layers: preheat the oven to 250°. Beat together the egg whites, salt, and cream of tartar until stiff. Gradually beat in 1 cup (240 milliliters) of sugar and continue to beat until meringue is stiff and glossy.

Line baking sheets with waxed paper and trace 3 circles (each 8 inches or 20.32 centimeters in diameter) on the paper. Spread the meringue evenly over the circles, about 1/4 inch (.64 centimeter) thick, and bake in the oven for 20-25 minutes, or until meringue is pale gold but still pliable. Remove from the oven and carefully peel the waxed paper from the bottom. Place on cake racks and dry.

To prepare the filling: in a double boiler, melt the chocolate pieces in water over hot water. Whip the cream until stiff. Gradually add the remaining sugar and beat until very stiff.

To assemble the dish: place a meringue layer on a serving plate and spread it with a thin covering of melted chocolate. Then, spread a layer about 3/4 inch (1.9 centimeters) thick of the whipped cream, and then top with a layer of sliced strawberries. Put a second layer of meringue on top, spread with chocolate, another layer of whipped cream and sliced strawberries. Top with the third layer of meringue. Frost the sides smoothly with the remaining whipped cream. Decorate the top meringue layer in an informal pattern, using the remaining melted chocolate squeezed through a pastry cone with a tiny round opening. (Or, decorate with whole ripe strawberries.) Refrigerate for 2 hours before serving.

Serves: 8

Top of the Park Restaurant

Proprietor: Stuart M. Levin

One Gulf & Western Plaza
New York, New York 10023
(212) 333-3800

The **Top of the Park Restaurant** combines spectacle, scenery, and delightful dining on excellent international cuisine in a stunning setting 43 floors above Central Park at the top of the Gulf & Western Building. A special experience begins as you enter the luxurious, softly lit dining room, with its deep blue decor and great expanse of glass affording a breathtaking view of the park and city below.

This is a good restaurant for confirmed pre-dinner nibblers; there's an oversized harvest basket set before you that contains stalks of celery, scallions, radishes, and whole green peppers, all accompanied by a curry dip.

My favorite house specialty—and there are several—is Escalope of Veal à la Viennoise, thinly sliced veal dipped in fresh bread crumbs, then sautéed in brown butter, topped with chopped eggs, minced parsley, and capers, and served with buttered spaetzle.

The Top of the Park Roast Duckling à l'Orange is one of the best I've tasted. They roast the Long Island Duckling to just the right degree of crispness and brush it with an orange sauce made with sugar, vinegar, sliced oranges, and Grand Marnier. It's served with nutted brown rice. The Washington State Silver Side Salmon—a whole, boned, poached salmon filled with a mousse of shrimp, bread crumbs, and fine herbs, and served with Mousseline sauce and Red Bliss potatoes—is an unusual seafood treat.

You can dine at Top of the Park often and continue to have new entrées since owner Stuart Levin tours regularly and returns with new recipes. Do sample the Chocolate Cake with Apricot Preserves for dessert or the Lemon Mousse Pie, Pineapple Cake with Kirsch and Toasted Coconut, or Rum Raisin Cream Crepe. They are also superb.

Top of the Park is open for dinner Monday through Saturday. Reservations are recommended, particularly for tables by the window. Gentlemen will need jackets and ties. All major credit cards are honored. Prices are moderate to moderately expensive.

CURRY DIP FOR CRUDITE

2 medium onions minced very finely

1 pint (470 milliliters) sour cream

2 pints (940 milliliters) heavy cream

1/2 pound (227 grams) cottage cheese

6 tablespoons (90 milliliters) curry powder, Cross & Blackwell preferred

1/2 teaspoon (2.5 milliliters) salt

In a mixing bowl, blend all of the above ingredients until the mixture has reached a smooth and creamy consistency. Cover the bowl and refrigerate.

It is best to make this curry dip at least one day in advance and two days in advance if possible. Serve with cut vegetables such as carrots, broccoli, celery, cauliflower, etc.

Serves: 8-10

The **"21" Club** has a legendary reputation in the international world of big business, sports, and politics. For the many leading figures who have been regular patrons for years and years, as well as for those "lesser mortals" who from time to time gain admittance, it is considered the leading status symbol in a city full of status and symbols.

Formerly a speakeasy, it is still a watering hole for the famous, but they also do serve good food. Entrées feature game bird dishes and, they have an extensive wine cellar. Goujonette of Sole is served in the lavish "21" manner, as are other seafood choices such as Filet of Lemon Sole Poche au Champagne; English Sole Poche, Margueray; Soft Shell Crab Sauté, Royer; and Swordfish Steak Grille, Stanley. A separate dessert menu offers many pastry, ice cream, and fruit and cheese selections.

There are two floors—downstairs a classy barroom with checked tablecloths; upstairs, white linen and haute cuisine service. Apparently where you sit really matters, but I can't remember the precise pecking order. The main thing is this is the gathering place for the rich and powerful who tend to use their meals as extensions of their business activities. It is not exactly restful, but for some it is mighty impressive.

"21" is open daily for lunch, dinner, and supper. Reservations are necessary. Correct, conservative dress is the rule, with jackets and ties required for gentlemen. Major credit cards are honored. Prices are expensive.

"21" Club

21 West 52nd Street
New York, New York 10019
(212) 582-7200

Chef: Anthony Pedretti

MUSHROOMS À LA DAUM

2 cups (480 milliliters) sliced mushrooms

1 cup (240 milliliters) minced onions

1 cup (240 milliliters) Danish ham and/or tongue, julienne

salt and freshly ground black pepper, to taste

8 tablespoons (120 milliliters) sweet butter

1/4 cup (60 milliliters) brown sauce (recipe follows)

fresh parsley, to garnish

4 tablespoons (60 milliliters) all-purpose flour

1 clove garlic, peeled

1 bay leaf

1/2 teaspoon (2.5 milliliters) dried chopped thyme

1 small onion, chopped

1/4 teaspoon (1.25 milliliters) Worcestershire sauce

Madeira wine, to taste

salt and freshly ground black pepper, to taste

In a mixing bowl, combine the mushrooms, onions, ham and/or tongue, and seasonings. Melt the butter in a skillet and sauté the mushroom mixture until the mushrooms and onions are soft. Stirring in the brown sauce, heat for 1 more minute. Serve over toast or prepared artichoke bottoms. Garnish with parsley.

Serves: 4

Brown Sauce

5 cups (1.2 liters) strong beef stock

4 tablespoons (60 milliliters) unsalted butter

Preheat the oven to 350°. Bring the stock to a boil. In a small heavy-bottomed saucepan, melt the butter and add the flour, blending thoroughly with a whisk, to make a roux. Allow the roux to cook for a few minutes until the mixture is slightly browned. Pour the stock into a casserole dish and stir in the roux. Simmer over low heat until the stock is slightly thickened. Add the garlic, bay leaf, thyme, onion, and Worcestershire sauce, and place the casserole in the oven. Roast for about 1 1/2 hours. Strain the sauce into a bowl or pan, add the wine, and season to taste with salt and pepper.

Yields: 1 quart (.95 liter)

Windows on the World is really three restaurants: *Windows on the World* (the main dining room), *Hors d'Oeuvrerie,* and *The Cellar in the Sky.*

The Cellar in the Sky is a small, romantic dining room. It is the working wine cellar for the entire restaurant. A single seven-course menu is adjusted every two weeks. The restaurant is open six days a week and formal wear is required.

The *Hors d'Oeuvrerie* is a separate place, "built for romance" around the City Lights Bar. Drinks and hors d'oeuvres are served between 3 p.m. and 1 a.m., with music beginning at 4:30, dancing at 7:30.

Windows on the World is the main attraction of the World Trade Center's dining complex. Because the dining room is built on many terraces, each table has an unobstructed view of the city. A buffet is served from noon until three on Saturday, and on

Sunday from noon until seven. Both buffets are steals at $14.95. The dining specialties are Rack of Young Lamb, James Beard; Rainbow Trout Stuffed and Baked in Pastry; and Scandinavian Steak Sauté with Dill and Horseradish. The pastry desserts are among the finest available in New York. Try the Golden Lemon Tart or the Hazelnut Dacquoise.

This restaurant also offers a table d'hote menu of four courses and an à la carte menu as well.

The service staff is young, friendly, and drawn from the world over. Alan Lewis, director of the entire complex, is proud to say that they speak 11 languages among them.

Dress is formal, and for a dining experience of this magnitude, prices are quite reasonable. All major credit cards are accepted.

Windows
on the World

One World Trade Center,
107th Floor
New York, New York 10048
(212) 938-1100

Director: Alan Lewis
Chef: Henry Boubee

THE GOLDEN LEMON TART

1 1/2 cups (360 milliliters) flour

pinch of salt

1/2 cup (120 milliliters) cold butter or shortening, cut in small pieces

4 tablespoons (60 milliliters) cold water

2 tablespoons (30 milliliters) cornstarch

1 1/2 cups (360 milliliters) water, approximately

5 egg yolks

1/2 cup (120 milliliters) strained fresh lemon juice

1/2 cup (114 grams) granulated sugar

1 tablespoon (15 milliliters) unsalted butter

1 teaspoon (5 milliliters) unflavored gelatin

1/2 cup (120 milliliters) heavy sweet cream, whipped

4 dry Italian macaroons (amaretti), crushed

1/2 cup (120 milliliters) apricot jam

2 large lemons, thinly sliced

To prepare the pastry: mix the flour and salt with the butter pieces by rubbing the butter and flour through the palms of the hands until all butter and flour are mixed. Pour water into the center of the mixture in a bowl and mix by hand until the dough forms a ball. (This should happen very quickly. Do not overwork.)

Lightly flour a surface and rolling pin. Roll out the dough 1/4 inch (.64 centimeter) thick. Line a 9-inch (23-centimeter) quiche pan or flan ring with the dough, pressing it into corners and sides. Chill for 20 minutes.

Line the unbaked shell with aluminum foil and fill with dried beans or rice. Bake in a preheated 350° oven until the crust is golden brown, about 25 minutes. Remove beans or rice and foil and allow the pastry to cool.

To prepare the filling: dissolve cornstarch in 1/4 cup (60 milliliters) water. Add egg yolks and mix thoroughly. Set aside.

In a saucepan, combine lemon juice, 2/3 cup (160 milliliters) water, and sugar. Bring to a boil. Add 1/4 cup (60 milliliters) of the hot liquid to the egg yolk mixture, constantly stirring. Next, add the egg yolk mixture to the hot lemon mixture and continue to stir. Return to a boil and boil for 3 minutes. Remove from heat. Stir in butter. Refrigerate.

Dissolve gelatin in 1/4 cup (60 milliliters) water over boiling water. Fold gelatin into the lemon mixture, which should be cool throughout, mixing thoroughly. Next, fold in the whipped cream and add crushed macaroons.

To assemble the tart: fill the pie shell with the filling. Melt the apricot jam with a little water and keep warm. Starting from the outside edge, cover the top of the tart with lemon slices dipped in jam.

Serves: 6-8

La

La Capannina brings to its service and food preparations the thoroughly professional attitude of its experienced owners and staff.

Appetizers such as Coktail di Gamberetti — tiny pink shrimps in a pink, parsley-studded sauce made of garlic and tomato in a rich fish stock; Pepata di Cozze — briny, sweet mussels in white wine; hot antipasto; Les Escargots Louis XIV; Vongole Posillipo — steamed clams in broth; and Funghetti al Limone — uncooked mushrooms with lemon dressing — all set La Capannina apart from its competition.

For seafood lovers, there are the imaginative Scampi d'Orleans, which combines shrimps, herbs, ginger, and wine pernod; and Filetti di Sogliola Roberta, fillet of sole with mushrooms, wine, and lemon. The veal and chicken dishes are equally imaginative and tasty.

La Capannina's desserts are authentic Italian. The Torta di Ricotta cheesecake, Zabaglione for two, and Zuppa Inglese (a very rich Italian version of English trifle) transport you to a Roman piazza. Coffee Royal is a treat and a delicious way to close out your meal.

Here is a restaurant that extends itself in the choice of dishes it prepares and does not disappoint even the most sophisticated palate.

La Capannina is open every day for dinner only. Make reservations. All major credit cards are honored. Prices are moderate.

Capannina

688 Fort Salonga Road
Northport, New York 11768
(516) 261-1188

Proprietors:
Giorgio Zavagnin and Renato Beneforti
Chef: Joseph Tudisco

VITELLO MILLEFIORI

flour, to dust

1 pound (454 grams) veal, sliced and pounded thinly

6 tablespoons (90 milliliters) vegetable oil

2 ounces (56 grams) Prosciutto ham, julienne

3 1/2 ounces (98 grams) butter

8 medium-sized fresh mushrooms, sliced thinly

1/2 cup (120 milliliters) shallots, chopped finely

8 canned artichoke hearts, quartered

2 half pimentos, cut in strips

pepper, to taste

1 1/2 ounces (45 milliliters) Chablis wine

veal or chicken stock, as needed

3 cups (720 milliliters) heavy cream

1/4 ounce (7.5 milliliters) brandy

Flour the veal lightly on both sides, then brown in hot vegetable oil in a heavy skillet. Remove the veal and discard the oil. Do not wash the pan.

In the same skillet, cook the Prosciutto for about 1 minute, then add butter, mushrooms, shallots, artichoke hearts, and pimentos. Season with pepper. Add the Chablis and a small amount of veal stock (enough to thin the sauce slightly). Cook until sauce becomes smooth.

Add the cream and cook slowly for about 5 minutes. Then add brandy, heat, and flame, then serve.

Serves: 4

Wine: *White*

During the last two decades, **Royal's Hearthside Restaurant** has become a landmark in the picturesque town of Rutland, Vermont. This totally restored 117-year-old white clapboard New England house with its warmly decorated interior of oak paneling, carved wood, large windows, stained glass, and open beam ceilings is the offspring of a partnership formed 45 years ago by Ernie and Willa Royal. The benefit of their years of restaurant experience (he as a chef and waiter, she as a baker, both in many of Boston's fine eateries) is self-evident in their success with the Hearthside, which today continues to offer area visitors and residents fine New England cuisine in a relaxed atmosphere.

One of the first things you'll notice at Royal's Hearthside Restaurant is the many homemade bakery items that accompany dinner or that can be purchased to take home. In fact, there is a separate area where you can drool over all the marvelous pastries, poppyseed, rye, and banana nut breads, and raisin and bran muffins. Live Maine lobster and prime rib highlight the entrée list that also features seasonally available fish and numerous meat dishes. Sweet, creamy clam chowder, excellent mock Caesar salad, homemade cole slaw, hot popovers, a choice of colloquial puddings (such as baked Indian or plum), followed by a cup of specially blended and ground coffee round out a superb meal that you're sure to remember.

Royal's Hearthside Restaurant is normally open daily from 11 a.m. to 10 p.m. A call for reservations is suggested. Major credit cards are welcomed. Prices are moderate.

Royal's Hearthside Restaurant

37 North Main Street
Rutland, Vermont
(802) 775-0856

Proprietor: Ernie Royal

HEARTHSIDE FISH CHOWDER

3-4 pounds (1.4-1.8 kilograms) small, whole haddock, filleted, head and skin removed, bones reserved

2 quarts (1.9 liters) water

1 ounce (28 grams) salt

1/4 pound (114 grams) grated or ground onion

2 pounds (900 grams) thinly sliced potatoes

5 ounces (140 grams) small diced salt pork, rinsed and drained

1 pint (470 milliliters) medium cream sauce, prepared

salt, to taste

1/2 ounce (14 grams) white pepper

1/4 ounce (7 grams) ground thyme

1 pint (470 milliliters) heavy cream

2 ounces (56 grams) butter

Place haddock fillets and bones in a shallow pan or casserole and cover with 1 1/2 quarts (1.5 liters) of water and the 1 ounce (28 grams) salt, and poach in a 375° oven for 25-30 minutes, or until the fish is tender but not overcooked. Set aside.

Cover the onions with the remaining water and boil until tender, about 10 minutes. Boil the sliced potatoes until tender, drain, and set aside.

Brown the diced salt pork in a frying pan. Remove the browned pieces of pork as they rise to the top of the hot fat and drain on absorbent paper. Discard the rendered fat.

In a large pot, stir the stock from the poached fish and the cream sauce together until smooth. (The consistency should be that of cream.) Add the boiled onions, seasonings, and stir again. Add the poached fish (discard the bones), boiled sliced potatoes, heavy cream, salt pork, and butter. Stir very gently so as not to break up the fish and potatoes. Heat to near boiling. Serve very hot with crackers.

Serves: 6-8

Wine: *Riesling*

arkansas

florida

georgia

louisianna

south carolina

tennessee

texas

Southern Region

Little Rock, Arkansas, does not usually come to mind as a place to enjoy fine Continental food, but **Restaurant Jacques & Suzanne** may help to change the image.

First of all, it's situated atop the tallest building in the state of Arkansas. From the thirtieth floor of the First National Bank Building the views over the Arkansas River are beautiful. The interior of Jacques & Suzanne is a pleasure to dine in. A large crystal chandelier is the center of attention in a dining room executed in Louis XIV-style. Beige linen and handsome silver appoint the tables.

Emince de Veau Zurichoise is a delicate Swiss specialty, but the original Escargot Jacques & Suzanne, Chateaubriand Escoffier, and Seafood Cardinal are French preparations. The wine list at Jacques & Suzanne includes domestic and imported selections in all price ranges. There is bar service as well as an adjacent cocktail lounge.

Chef/Manager Paul Bash is a true restaurant professional. In addition to his practical experience, he holds a Bachelor's degree in Restaurant Management from Michigan State University and a Master's degree in business from the University of Michigan, but more important, he trained in Montreal, Brussels, and Geneva. With Mr. Bash overseeing the service and menu, Jacques & Suzanne seems assured of continuing success and even more awards than it's garnered since opening in 1975.

Jackets are required evening wear for gentlemen, reservations are recommended, and all major credit cards are honored. Jacques & Suzanne is open for lunch and dinner Tuesday through Saturday. Prices are moderately expensive.

Restaurant Jacques & Suzanne

First National Bank Building
Capitol and Broadway
Little Rock, Arkansas 72201
(501) 376-6616

Chef: Paul Bash

ESCARGOTS JACQUES & SUZANNE

1/2 ounce (14 grams) finely chopped garlic

1/2 ounce (14 grams) finely chopped shallots

1 1/2 ounces (42 grams) finely chopped parsley

1/2 anchovy fillet, finely chopped

1 filbert, chopped

14 ounces (420 milliliters) unsalted butter

2 1/2 teaspoons (12.5 milliliters) salt

pinch of white pepper

pinch of cayenne pepper

juice of 1/4 lemon

1 teaspoon (5 milliliters) Pernod

2 teaspoons (10 milliliters) dry white wine

24 snails

1 1/2 cups (360 milliliters) dry white wine

3/4 cup (180 milliliters) whipping cream

1/2 cup (120 milliliters) whipped cream

To prepare escargot butter: place the garlic, shallots, parsley, anchovy fillet, and filbert in a blender and blend thoroughly.

In a separate mixing bowl, beat the butter with the salt and peppers until well incorporated with air. Add the puréed mixture from the blender, the lemon juice, the Pernod, and white wine and continue beating.

Place the escargot butter in a covered container and refrigerate for several days. (Butter can also be frozen.) For service, butter should be at room temperature.

Heat the snails in dry white wine, then place in escargot dishes.

Reduce the whipping cream by half. Remove from heat and, when it is tepid, use a French whip and mix in the soft (room temperature) escargot butter, piece by piece. Fold in the whipped cream.

Pour the butter-cream mixture over the snails and glaze them quickly under the broiler until golden. Suggestion: serve with crusty French bread.

Serves: 4

Wine: *Chablis Premier Cru or Pinot Chardonnay*

Maison & Jardin Restaurant

Proprietor: William R. Beuret
Chef: Hans Spirig

430 South Wymore Road
Altamonte Springs, Florida 32701
(305) 862-4410

At **Maison & Jardin Restaurant**, the decor and ambiance are as much a treat to the eye as the exemplary Continental offerings are to the palate. Elegant formal dining takes place in a luxurious Mediterranean-style villa set on the side of a hill. Roman statuary and wrought iron tables with Cinzano umbrellas grace the area.

What awaits you inside is chic, inviting, exciting. The Patio Room is furnished with bamboo and wicker chairs, hanging greenery, and yellow tablecloths. The Terrace Room is airy, light, and very French. The Gazebo Room is an intimate dining area overlooking a formal garden and fountains. Here the tablecloths are delft blue, the flowers are yellow daisies.

Before you enjoy what Swiss chef Hans Spirig has prepared, there is a very extensive wine list.

Exploration of the very interesting menu reveals appetizers on the order of Blinis à la Russe, a rich and hearty favorite; Mushrooms Thermidor; and Oysters Florentine au Gratin.

Salads are much more than the usual routine greenery at Maison & Jardin, as is evidenced by the success of their unusual Famous Fresh Spinach Salad.

Proprietor William Beuret recommends the Veal Strassbourg entrée. Another popular veal selection is the Veal Oscar. From their own aging room comes U.S.D.A. prime western beef in the form of Filet of Beef Wellington, Filet Mignon Café de Paris, Entrecôte Foyot, and a particularly fine Filet Mignon Hotel Olympic, among others.

Elegant desserts and special coffees help end your dinner on the right note.

Maison & Jardin serves dinner every night but Monday. A New Orleans Sunday Brunch with live Dixieland jazz is held the first Sunday of every month. Reservations are advised. Jackets are required. Major credit cards are honored. Prices are moderate to expensive.

VEAL STRASSBOURG

12 3-ounce (84-gram) veal cutlets

6 ounces (168 grams) pâté de foie gras

salt and pepper, to taste

flour, to dredge

butter, to sauté

1 quart (.95 liter) Morel Sauce (*recipe follows*)

Pound the veal cutlets thin, but not too thin. Stuff pâté between two cutlets per portion. Sprinkle with salt and pepper and dredge in flour.

Sauté the cutlets in butter on both sides for approximately 3 minutes per side. Place on a serving platter and ladle the Morel Sauce over each portion. Garnish appropriately and serve additional sauce on the side.

Morel Sauce

2 ounces (56 grams) dried morels

butter, to sauté

2 tablespoons (30 milliliters) chopped shallots

2 ounces (60 milliliters) brandy

1 quart (.95 liter) heavy whipping cream

1 tablespoon (15 milliliters) meat glaze

2 tablespoons (30 milliliters) roux

salt and pepper, to taste

Soak the morels for 1/2 hour in water, then drain. Repeat with fresh water. Strain well and cut the morels in half. Wash again two more times to be sure all grit is removed. Drain well.

Sauté the morels in butter as hot as possible without burning. Add the chopped shallots and brandy, and flame. Add the cream and reduce for 10 minutes.

Add the meat glaze and roux and season to taste. Cook for another 15 minutes until smooth, stirring with a spoon.

Yields: 1 quart (.95 liter)

Wine: *California Chardonnay or a fine White Burgundy*   Serves: 6

Mai-Kai Restaurant

Proprietor: Robert F. Thornton

3599 North Federal Highway
Fort Lauderdale, Florida 33308
(305) 563-3272

Mai-Kai Restaurant features alluring south seas landscaping, totally authentic Polynesian decor and atmosphere; it is an enchanting world apart. The restaurant and grounds resemble a native village, with thatch-roof huts, ancient carvings, lush tropical plantings, waterfalls, lagoons, and 40-foot Tikis. Owner Bob Thornton has made many trips throughout the Pacific and the Orient, conducting extensive research in cuisine and decor, and returning with additional decorative items and menu ideas to enhance Mai-Kai's unique ambiance and culinary reputation.

Looking like a south seas waterfront saloon of clipper ship days, the Molokai Bar offers a variety of exclusive and exotic tropical concoctions and almost continuous music. Each of the eight dining rooms is named after a different Pacific island group and is appropriately decorated. Visible to diners are three huge Chinese smoke ovens inside a glass-enclosed pagoda. Here a dozen entrées, ranging from filet mignon and sirloin strip to rack of lamb

and Peking duck, are cooked to a flavorful tenderness in the smoke of burning oak and pine logs.

The Mai-Kai's many varieties of elegant Cantonese dishes are artistically prepared and served with Polynesian flair. In addition to the popular pu-pu platter, the chef takes special and well-deserved pride in his original creations—Shrimp Lee Lin Ark and, a favorite of mine, boned, roasted duck in ginger sauce. Another popular dish is Chicken Mai-Kai which consists of chopped chunks of chicken breasts and bean sprouts sautéed with mushrooms, onions, and Chinese vegetables. It is light and flavorful and healthy.

Open each day for dinner, Mai-Kai presents a nightly native show of pulse-pounding island music and dance performed by beautiful and talented girls from Tahiti, Samoa, and Hawaii, and directed by Mireil from Tahiti, who is also Mrs. Thornton. Reservations are a necessity. Casual attire is welcome, and major credit cards are accepted. Prices are moderate.

SCALLOPS SINGAPORE

2 tablespoons (30 milliliters) peanut oil

1/2 teaspoon (2.5 milliliters) salt

10 ounces (280 grams) bay scallops, well drained

1 inch (2.54 centimeter) slice fresh ginger root, smashed and chopped

7-8 large fresh mushrooms, sliced into thirds

1/2 tablespoon (7.5 milliliters) sherry wine

1/2 cup (120 milliliters) chicken broth

1 tablespoon (15 milliliters) oriental oyster sauce, or use soy sauce

1/2 teaspoon (2.5 milliliters) MSG

1 green onion, shredded

1 tablespoon (15 milliliters) cornstarch, or as needed

Heat the peanut oil in a wok over medium high heat and add salt. To the hot oil, add the scallops and ginger root. Stir briefly, then add mushrooms and sherry and stir to prevent burning. Add chicken broth, oyster sauce, and MSG. Cover and simmer for about 30 seconds. Add the green onion and enough cornstarch to slightly thicken the mixture. Remove from heat immediately.

Serve as an appetizer or as a main entrée.

Serves: 2

Far Horizons Beach Resort offers a luxurious restaurant with quiet, elegant dining on Continental and American specialties. The atmosphere is both chic and relaxing, with a blue/green decor accented by tropical rattan furniture. Soft music by harpist James Kirk is conducive to the enjoyment of good eating.

Dinner begins with careful reading of the extensive international wine list and continues with serious sampling of the appetizers— among them the hot Escargot de Bourgogne, Gulf Shrimp Provençale, the cold Pâté de Foie Maison, and Smoked Nova Scotia Salmon Garni. For soup, turn to Spanish Gazpacho Supreme or Bisque of Shrimp with Sherry wine.

You would expect to find excellent seafood in such a location, and you do, such as Florida Silver Pompano Mirabeaux—a broiled pompano filet garnished with olives, anchovies, and herb butter. The Alaskan King Crab Meat de luxe Mornay is slowly simmered in seasoned Béchamel, sprinkled with grated Parmesan cheese, and browned under the broiler.

If you must have beef, try Filet Mignon aux Champignons, Grilled New York Cut Sirloin, Escalope de Veau Florentine, or tasty versions of an old fashioned Corned Brisket of New York Beef with cabbage and parsley potatoes.

Rich desserts for the sweet-toothed include Far Horizons Cheesecake, Georgia Pecan Pie, Florida Key Lime Pie, Peche Melba, Pear Belle-Helene, and Mousse au Chocolat.

Far Horizons serves breakfast, lunch and dinner daily. Reservations are recommended. Gentlemen are asked to wear jackets for dinner. Major credit cards are honored. Prices are moderate.

Far Horizons Beach Resort

2401 Gulf of Mexico Drive
Sarasota, Florida 33548
(813) 383-2441

Chef: Harold Wuelfrath

FRESH GULF POMPANO OSTENDAISE

4 6-ounce (168-gram) fillets of
  pompano, boneless and skinless

8 shrimp

8 large oysters

8 large mushroom caps

  pinch of chives

4 chopped shallots

1 bay leaf

  juice of 1 lemon

2 ounces (60 milliliters) butter

2 ounces (60 milliliters) white wine

4 cups (950 milliliters) water

butter and flour, to thicken

2 egg yolks, beaten

1 cup (240 milliliters) whipped
  cream

Simmer the first 11 ingredients together for 12 minutes, then remove the fish and garniture from the broth and place on an ovenproof baking dish. Thicken the broth with butter and flour, add the egg yolks and whipped cream, and pour over the fish. Broil until a golden brown.

Serves: 4

Wine: *Vin des "Coteaux Champenois Blanc Lanson"*

the Fields' Buccaneer

Proprietors: The Field Family

595 Dream Island Road
Longboat Key, Florida
(813) 383-5565

Longboat Key is located off the west coast of the Florida peninsula in the Gulf of Mexico. Across the bay is Sarasota. This area is the winter home of northern tourists, baseball teams, and the Ringling Bros. circus, as well as the permanent home of many fine year-round attractions—not the least of which is **The Buccaneer Inn,** owned and operated by the Field family since its inception 24 years ago. In addition to the spacious accommodations, a visit to the Buccaneer Inn will reveal a bustling yacht harbor and marina, lighted tennis courts, swimming pools, and last, but not least, a marvelous award-winning restaurant that should not be missed.

This restaurant offers a quiet, cheerful nautical atmosphere that is intended to reflect the area's buccaneer heritage. (It is believed that infamous pirates such as Jean Laffitte, Blackbeard, and Henry Morgan actually gathered on this key to feast on the food and grog of their time.) The superbly prepared menu items of the Buccaneer Inn restaurant complement the decor perfectly. Whether the pirates actually enjoyed the same outstanding charcoal-broiled prime rib or baby back ribs is irrelevant. The point is that you think they did. These two entrées are very successfully prepared. The prime rib is roasted rare, then sliced, then bronzed over a charcoal fire to perfection. The baby back ribs are similarly broiled, but are basted eight hours with a homemade barbecue sauce. As unique and tasty as these two dishes are, you can be sure there are many more special treats available to you. Don't forget that the Buccaneer Inn is located right on one of the world's great fishing holes. Many variations of Gulf shrimp,

Inn

flounder, scallops, red snapper, and others await you. And to top off your dinner—the opportunity to create your own ice cream sundae.

The Fields' Buccaneer Inn is in a beautiful location that should be visited. Their restaurant should not be missed. It is open for lunch, Monday through Saturday; for dinner, seven nights a week. Dress is casual. Reservations are suggested and all major credit cards are accepted. Prices are moderately expensive.

HOUSE DRESSING

1 6-ounce (168-gram) can anchovies, ground medium

3 scallions, ground medium

1 pint (470 milliliters) salad dressing, prepared

1 pint (470 milliliters) sour cream

1/2 teaspoon (2.5 milliliters) white pepper

bit of pimento, chopped to please

Mix all the ingredients together well. Chill in a covered container and store in the refrigerator.

Yields: approximately 1 quart (.95 liter)

Joe's Stone Crab Restaurant

227 Biscayne Street
Miami Beach, Florida 33139
(305) 673-0365

Joe's Stone Crab Restaurant, the oldest restaurant in Miami Beach, remains first in the hearts of thousands of devotees of the tasty crustacean across the country and around the world. Joe's was first to recognize its culinary potential—developing it to a state of unequalled perfection. The popularity of the stone crab claws served at Joe's requires the services of a fleet of 30 boats, whose owners supply the restaurant with a million pounds of crabs annually.

This internationally-known institution has been owned and operated by members of the Weiss family for all of its 67 years. Their personalized management and genuine interest accounts for the uniquely warm, friendly atmosphere, and for Joe's enduring success. Heaping mounds of crab claws—source of the best meat—are served chilled and cracked with melted butter and lemon or a mustard sauce. Freshness is assured. No crab is served more than a day or two after being caught.

While stone crab is the specialty, the menu also presents an extensive and tempting array of seafood classics and American staples, such as pompano sautéed in garlic butter, Maine or Florida lobsters, fried shrimp in garlic butter, fried oysters, Spanish mackerel, filet of flounder or sole, and of course, steaks, chops, and chicken.

Joe's Stone Crab Restaurant has been designated an historical landmark by the Miami City Commission.

It is open for lunch and dinner, Monday through Friday, but only from October 15 to May 15 (the seven-month stone crab season). Reservations are not accepted. Jackets and ties, or sport clothes in good taste are preferred. Major credit cards are welcomed. Prices are moderate.

MUSTARD SAUCE

4 ounces (120 milliliters) Coleman's English mustard

1 quart (470 milliliters) mayonnaise

1/2 cup (120 milliliters) A1 sauce

1/2 cup (120 milliliters) Lea & Perrins Worcestershire sauce

4 ounces (120 milliliters) cream

In a bowl, combine the mustard, mayonnaise, A1 sauce, and Worcestershire sauce using a wire whisk. Beat until smooth. Slowly add the cream and continue to beat until you reach proper sauce consistency. Serve as a relish with cold fish or meats.

Sauce can be refrigerated for future use.

Yields: about 5 cups (1.2 liters)

Bern's Steak House

1208 South Howard Avenue
Tampa, Florida 33606
(813) 251-2421

Proprietor: Bern Laxer

Bern's Steak House has developed the cooking and serving of steak into an art form. The attention to detail, the maintenance of high quality standards, is carried out to a unique degree. Meat is aged five to eight weeks on the premises before a steak is cut to your order. Though most prefer the taste and tenderness of fine aged beef, fresher cuts are available for those who like their meat that way.

Steaks may be cooked very rare, rare, medium rare, medium, medium well, and well done, or something in between two degrees of doneness. Also to be noted are Broiled Shrimp and Scandinavian Lobster Tails, which are charcoal-broiled on skewers and basted with seasoned sweet butter.

Baked Alaska Bern is a flaming dessert prepared for two or more. There are ice creams (with a variety of fruit, nut, and liqueur top-pings), sherbets, pies, and parfaits. Cappuccino Bern's consists of fresh ground and roasted coffees, marinated in a blend of liqueurs four weeks, and served with a float of heavy cream. Cappuccino Ybor City is a Cuban-style coffee with liqueur and whipped cream. Eight teas are available singly or mixed in bags filled to Bern's specifications.

Bern's has its own farm, which is devoted to growing fresh vegetables and salad greens, and to producing eggs for the restaurant. Organic farming methods are followed, and no poison sprays or harmful chemicals are used. The list of quality maintenance standards and procedures seems to run on almost endlessly.

Bern's Steak House is open for dinner every night but Christmas Eve. Reservations are strongly recommended. Jackets and ties for men are preferred. Major credit cards are honored. Prices are expensive.

BRAZILIAN SNOW

4-6 rounded tablespoons (60-90 milliliters) fresh roasted coffee, unground

1 pint (470 milliliters) best quality vanilla ice cream

whipped cream, as needed

4 cherries, to garnish

Grind the coffee as finely as you can with a small nut grinder. Sprinkle about 1/4 of the coffee over the ice cream in the container. Scoop up one portion of ice cream, trying to mix the ice cream and ground coffee together without overhandling the ice cream, and place in a serving dish. Then, sprinkle more coffee over the ice cream in the container and continue to serve the ice cream-coffee mixture into dishes until all the ice cream is divided and only a scant teaspoonful of coffee remains.

Top each dish with whipped cream and sprinkle the last of the ground coffee over the whipped cream. Garnish with a cherry and serve at once. Remember: the coffee loses its flavor soon after it's ground. It shouldn't be consumed after 5 or 10 minutes if you want the maximum fresh coffee taste.

Serves: 4

the Abbey

Proprietor: William F. Swearingen
Chef: Hans J. Bertram

163 Ponce de Leon Avenue
Atlanta, Georgia 30308
(404) 876-8831

The first thing I want to point out about **The Abbey** is that it may have it all over other "theme" restaurants as far as authenticity is concerned. You see, this restaurant is a church, an old one built back in 1915 for the local Methodists and Episcopalians, but as the face of the city changed, this building gradually outlived its usefulness. Then, William Swearingen and his associates enterprisingly intervened and initiated a renaissance—a miraculous transformation of a derelict house of worship into a divine house of fine food.

The visual impact upon entering The Abbey is awesome—massive stained glass windows, huge 50-foot high arched vaulted ceilings, handcrafted woodwork—all that was there. What has changed? Well, the owners added beautiful tapestries and statuary and monks' chairs and copperware. Where pews once stood, now there are leather and dark wood dining ensembles. And they also added an ultra-modern kitchen facility and installed Chef Hans Bertram, who was originally trained in West Germany and, prior to coming to The Abbey in 1973, worked for several

of the best restaurants in Europe and South Africa.

The Abbey's menu is as imposing as its environment: a seemingly endless array of Continental dishes, highlighted by many specialties of some of Europe's finest establishments and by unique creations by Chef Bertram. It is one of the most all encompassing menus I know. Aside from the unique atmosphere, this is the perfect place to go when you're not sure what you feel like eating: chances are they've got it.

Meals are served by an excellent staff of waiters garbed in monks' frocks. The wine selection is extensive, as befitting an abbey, and the house wine is drawn from the Taylor California Cellars. This beautiful setting, the fine food, and good wine are made even more delightful by the unique strains of harp music lightly echoing through the sanctuary.

The Abbey is open for dinner seven days a week. Reservations are suggested. Dress is jackets for men and no jeans for anyone. All major credit cards are accepted. Prices are moderately expensive.

COLD MAINE LOBSTER À LA MAISON

1 1/2 cups (360 milliliters) mayonnaise

1/2 ounce (15 milliliters) cognac

finely shredded fresh horseradish, to taste

juice of 1/2 lemon

dash of Lea & Perrins Worcestershire sauce

salt and white pepper, to taste

1 ounce (30 milliliters) grapefruit juice

1 ounce (30 milliliters) tomato ketchup

3 grapefruit

2 heads Boston or Bibb lettuce

20 medallions poached cold Maine lobster

lobster heads, parsley, fresh flowers, and lemon slices, for decoration

To prepare the dressing: mix the mayonnaise with cognac, horseradish, lemon juice, Worcestershire sauce, salt, white pepper, grapefruit juice, and tomato ketchup. Refrigerate.

Cut 2 grapefruit in half, scoop out the inside sections, and cut the edges at an angle. Fill the center with clean lettuce leaves. Cut grapefruit sections from the remaining grapefruit. Place 5 lobster medallions, alternating with grapefruit sections, in the center of each grapefruit half.

To serve: set the filled grapefruit on an ice sockel (a mold with a flower in ice), which has been placed on a napkin on a plate. Place the lobster heads, parsley, fresh flowers, and lemon slices around the ice sockel. Pour the dressing over the medallions and grapefruit sections.

Serves: 4

Wine: *Spring Mountain Chardonnay, 1977*

Anthonys is the real thing, whether you're looking for the authentic ambiance of the old South, distinctive Continental cuisine with a light Southern touch—or both. You dine in the actual plantation mansion that Wiley Pope built in 1797. Located in the outskirts of Atlanta, this handsomely restored home offers dining in nine rooms, each decorated in its own traditional manner. You may choose the cozy brick kitchen with an open hearth fireplace downstairs, chandeliered 18th century parlors, a glass-enclosed veranda, a greenhouse bedecked with fresh flowers and plants, or the upstairs bedroom suites.

Anthonys provides your table with a complimentary bowl of shrimp. Cold appetizers include large Gulf shrimp in melon, Andalouse; and smoked Danish salmon with caviar. The hot items include: mushrooms stuffed with veal au gratin; three popular oyster dishes combined into one; and a casserole of escargots in Chablis.

Chef William Janousek recommends his "Pompano Charleston," which is pompano stuffed with crabmeat, hollandaise, and fleurons. Also interesting is his boneless capon and shrimp Creole, served in a ring of rice, or the Supreme of Pheasant, poached with pecans, raisins, and rice Panache. If this doesn't tempt you, try roasted and stuffed whole Maine lobster, Georgia quail, Chateaubriand Wellington for two, or Veal Anthony with shrimp and mushrooms. The well-chosen wine list displays many imported and domestic selections.

The menu also notes three prix fixe dinners at different price levels.

Anthonys serves dinner every night but Sunday. Reservations are most definitely advised. Jackets and ties are preferred. All major credit cards are welcomed. Prices range from medium to expensive.

Anthonys Restaurant

3109 Piedmont Road, N.E.
Atlanta, Georgia 30305
(404) 233-7129

Proprietor: A.J. Anthony
Chef: William Janousek

VEAL ANTHONY WITH SHRIMP AND MUSHROOMS

1 pound (454 grams) finely chopped or ground mushrooms

1/2 cup (120 milliliters) Madeira sauce, prepared

1 cup (240 milliliters) dry white wine

1/2 cup (120 milliliters) lemon juice

salt and pepper, to taste

3 3-ounce (84-gram) pieces of veal, flattened

3 butterfly shrimp, flattened

seasoned flour, as needed

cooking oil, to sauté

garlic butter, to sauté (optional)

Béarnaise Sauce (recipe follows)

chopped parsley to garnish

To prepare mushroom mixture: mix the mushrooms, Madeira sauce, salt and pepper together and cook for 3 minutes. Add the white wine and lemon juice. Cook and keep stirring until sauce is reduced and very thick. Correct the seasoning.

Drench both the veal and shrimp in seasoned flour. Sauté the veal, browning it quickly on both sides. Sauté the shrimp in garlic butter or bake it in the oven. Top each piece of veal with mushroom mixture, then set shrimp on top. Cover with Béarnaise Sauce and chopped parsley.

Béarnaise Sauce

1 cup (240 milliliters) tarragon white wine vinegar

12 medium-sized shallots, finely minced

2 teaspoons (10 milliliters) dried tarragon leaves

3 cups (720 milliliters) whipping cream

12 egg yolks

1 cup (240 milliliters) sweet butter, cut in pieces

salt and white pepper, to taste

Heat the vinegar, shallots, and tarragon in a saucepan until boiling. Boil to reduce the liquid to 4 tablespoons (60 milliliters), approximately 5 minutes. Stir in 2/3 the cream. Whisk in the egg yolks over low heat until the mixture begins to thicken. Vigorously whisk in the butter, one piece at a time. Whisk until the mixture is light and fluffy. Stir in the remaining cream. Strain, discard the solids, and season to taste with salt and white pepper.

This sauce can be kept warm in a double boiler or will keep refrigerated for 2 days then reheated in a double boiler.

Wine: *Pouilly Fumé*

Serves: 3

Bugatti Restaurant

Manager: Tino Venturi
Chef: Aniello Vellino

Omni International Hotel
Atlanta, Georgia
(404) 659-0000

Bugatti Restaurant serves Northern Italian food in a dignified yet very friendly atmosphere. The high-ceilinged dining room is quiet, attractive, and relaxing, with its dark woods, deep carpeting, hunter green velvet covered booths, and creamy brown leather chairs.

After selecting your wine from a list of well-known imported and domestic favorites, you will find cold appetizers such as: Frutti Di Mare Portofino—a delicately marinated seafood cocktail—or the more traditional Antipasto Italiano. Hot appetizers include Gamberetti Bagna Cauda (Piemontese shrimp with garlic and anchovy) and Impetata Di Cozze (mussels with pepper and garlic). For heartier fare, ideal choices are the soups Pasta e Fagioli (Italian red bean soup) and Stracciatella Alla Romana (spinach, egg, and Parmesan cheese soup).

What is an Italian dinner without pasta, particularly homemade pasta the likes of Spaghetti Marinara, Spaghetti Carbonara, and my fattening favorite, Fettucine Alfredo? All are delicious here.

The many fine entrées fresh from the sea are highlighted by the Zuppa Di Pesce, a variety of fish, shrimp and mussels in tomato sauce.

Other Bugatti house specialties cover a wide range of chicken, veal, and beef dishes, such as Petto di Pollo Villa D'Este (chicken breast with mushrooms and mozzarella cheese), Uccelletti di Vitello (veal strips flavored with rosemary, served in a dry white wine sauce), and Scaloppine Alla Ziagara (scaloppine with ham and mushrooms in Madeira sauce).

A dessert for two is a delicate Zabaglione al Marsala (a concoction of foamy eggs and Marsala cream). There is also an array of pastries, tarts, ice creams, and of course, fresh fruit with an ample cheese tray.

Bugatti serves breakfast, lunch, and dinner every day, as well as a popular brunch on Sunday. Reservations are advised. Gentlemen are asked to wear jackets. All major credit cards are honored. Prices are in the medium range.

ZUPPA DI PESCE
(Seafood Casserole)

3 ounces (90 milliliters) olive oil

3 cloves chopped garlic

3 tablespoons (45 milliliters) chopped onions

6 ounces (168 grams) clams

12 ounces (336 grams) mussels

3 ounces (84 grams) squid

15 ounces (420 grams) shrimp

3 ounces (90 milliliters) white wine

6 ounces (180 milliliters) fish stock

6 ounces (180 milliliters) tomato sauce

1 dash each: oregano, basil, salt, and pepper

6 ounces (168 grams) sea bass

6 drops Tabasco sauce, or to taste

Place the olive oil, garlic, and onions in a pot and sauté until tender. Add the clams and mussels. When they have opened, add the squid and shrimp and simmer together. Add the wine, let evaporate, then add the fish stock, tomato sauce, spices, salt, and pepper. Let this cook for 10 minutes, then add the sea bass. Let cook another 5 minutes, then add Tabasco to taste.

Serving suggestion: place the seafood in individual casseroles on top of two shells of clams and a slice of French bread toasted with garlic oil and chopped parsley. Serve very hot.

Serves: 6

The Coach and Six Restaurant, Inc. has, for almost 20 years, enjoyed a widespread reputation for the uncompromising quality of its good, solid American cooking. Much of their patronage is repeat business. A 25-foot mural hangs in the cocktail lounge bearing portraits in oil of more than 400 of those long-standing customers.

Seated in the warm, dark, comfortable atmosphere of an English club, you will probably want to start your dinner with their very rich Black Bean Soup or traditional French Onion Soup au Gratin. There is also a variety of shrimp, clam, crab, and oyster appetizers, all delicious.

The Steak au Poivre entrée is a full one-pound sirloin steak coated with freshly crushed black pepper, and served with cognac sauce. Another good bet is their special Steak Angelo, a thick filet mignon, served with sautéed fresh mushrooms, onions, green peppers, and hash brown potatoes. Lobster Alfaro is very special too. It consists of chunks of imported lobster tail with breast of chicken, shallots, and sautéed in a delicate sherry wine and almond sauce, with rice pilaf.

Pastries and other desserts are baked daily on the premises by Pastry Chef Ernest Duersteler. These desserts include a very light-textured Chocolate Mousse, a creamy French cheese cake, and Strawberries Romanoff. And try a steaming mug of Irish Coffee.

Luncheon is served weekdays at the Coach and Six, and dinner is served every day. Reservations are recommended. Jackets for gentlemen are required. All major credit cards are honored. Prices range from medium to expensive.

Coach and Six Restaurant, Inc.

1776 Peachtree Road, N.W.
Atlanta, Georgia 30309
(404) 872-6666

BLACK BEAN SOUP

4 cups (960 milliliters) black beans, washed

cold water, as needed

5 quarts (4.75 liters) cold water

3 stalks celery

3 large onions, finely chopped

1/2 cup (120 milliliters) butter

2 1/2 tablespoons (37.5 milliliters) flour

1/2 cup (120 milliliters) finely chopped parsley

rind and bone of 1 cooked smoked ham

3 leeks, thinly sliced

4 bay leaves

1 tablespoon (15 milliliters) salt

1/2 teaspoon (2.5 milliliters) freshly ground black pepper

1 cup (240 milliliters) dry Madeira wine

2 finely chopped hard-cooked eggs

thin lemon slices, to garnish

Soak the black beans overnight in enough cold water to cover them, then drain. Add 5 quarts (4.75 liters) cold water and cook the beans over low heat for 1 1/2 hours.

In a soup kettle over low heat, sauté the celery and onions in butter for about 8 minutes or until they are tender. Blend in the flour and chopped parsley and cook the mixture, stirring, for 1 minute. Gradually stir in the beans and their liquid. Add the rind and bone of the ham, leeks, bay leaves, salt and pepper. Simmer the soup for 4 hours.

Remove and discard the hambone, rind, and bay leaves, and force the beans through a sieve. Mix the puréed beans with their broth and add the Madeira wine. Heat the soup, then remove it from the heat and stir in the eggs. Float a thin slice of lemon on each serving.

Serves: 14-16

Hugo's in the Hyatt Regency Atlanta Hotel presents an atmosphere of formal elegance that is very welcome in a city that is full of "come as you are" casual restaurants.

You'll notice a four-tiered dessert cart just inside the entrance which is an indication of things to come. Candlelight, roses, crystal, and gold-rimmed china adorn the comfortably-sized dining room. There are luxurious leather padded booths, too. The wine list is extensive; there are over 120 offerings exclusive of cognac, sherry, champagne, apéritifs and the like. You may assume correctly that the food matches the wine list. It is really very good. The service is friendly but formal. A harpist plays through the night.

Chef William Fontes, who began his European training at the age of 14, prepares such excellent dishes as "boula-boula" soup composed of cream of turtle and pea soups laced with Tio Pepe sherry and topped with heavy cream and a sweetbreads entrée prepared with truffles, Madeira, and mushrooms. One of the selections from the dessert cart is a cake made up of three chocolates varying in sweetness and heaviness. All the food is imaginatively prepared and served with the grace and dignity we would expect to find in a first class restaurant.

Manager Daniel Senne worked in London and Paris before becoming maître d' at a fine restaurant in New York. His efforts here have helped make Hugo's one of the finest restaurants in Atlanta.

Hugo's is open seven days a week for dinner only. Seating is limited, so do make reservations. All major credit cards are accepted. Prices are expensive.

Hugo's

Hyatt Regency Atlanta Hotel
265 Peachtree Street, N.E.
Atlanta, Georgia 30301
(404) 577-1234

RIS DE VEAU FINACIÈRE
(Veal Sweetbreads With Madeira)

court-bouillon of white mirepoix, prepared, enough to poach

2 6-ounce (168-gram) portions of veal sweetbreads, peeled and trimmed of skin and veins

1 cup (240 milliliters) demi-glaze

1 cup (240 milliliters) mushroom stems or trimmings

1/4 cup (60 milliliters) Madeira wine

butter, as needed

1/4 cup (60 milliliters) Creme Fraiche, or heavy cream

salt and pepper, to taste

flour, to dust

oil, to sauté

4 green asparagus, cut 3 inches (7.6 centimeters) from the tip

1 1-ounce (28-gram) truffle, Black Perigord preferred

In the court-bouillon, poach the sweetbreads for 10 minutes until slightly firm. Remove them from the poaching liquid and press them between two pie pans, using a weight, for 20 minutes.

While the sweetbreads are poaching, mix the demi-glaze, mushrooms, and Madeira together. Simmer and reduce by half. Strain and place in a bain-marie. Float a small piece of butter on top of the Madeira sauce to prevent a skin from forming.

Reduce the Creme Fraiche by half to a glossy, pearl-white color, to make double cream.

Cut the two portions of sweetbreads into 3 medallions each. Season with salt and pepper and dust with flour. Sauté until golden brown. In the same skillet, roll the asparagus tips to heat them.

Coat the bottom of a heated platter with the Madeira sauce, arrange the medallions on the sauce, nap with double cream, top with asparagus tips and truffle slice, and serve. Suggestion: serve with wild rice and fresh garden vegetables.

Serves: 2

Wine: *Beaujolais Villages*

La Grotta Ristorante Italiano

Proprietors: Sergio Favalli and
Antonio Pecondon

2637 Peachtree Road, N.E.
Atlanta, Georgia 30305
(404) 231-1368

La Grotta Ristorante Italiano isn't big. It doesn't have any romantic history because it's not very old. It doesn't have any fountains or any valet parking. It's even hard to find—it's underneath an apartment building. But, nevertheless, find it! Go there! It's worth more than all the fountains and history of many other restaurants because of two things: La Grotta has spirit and authenticity.

The spirit is generated by Sergio Favalli and Antonio Pecondon, the owners, and is manifested in the form of boundless enthusiasm for and bursting pride in their endeavor. Sergio has worked all over Europe as well as in the Caribbean and the U.S. and obviously has a great deal of experience at making people comfortable while dining. Antonio, in addition to being part-owner, is also the chef. He received his formal and practical training in Europe. Antonio prepares authentic northern Italian cuisine—delicate sauces rich with the scents of fresh herbs and spices served on homemade and imported pasta—beef tenderloin marinated for five hours in rosemary, basil, shallots, mustard, and lemon juice—and the veal, ah! the veal, cooked to perfection, never rushed, always tender—served with a good bottle of *vino Italiano* and, unlike after eating heavy southern Italian cooking, you still have room for a marvelous dessert specialty.

I hope this two-year-old restaurant will stay around for generations. In time, it will have its history and maybe a fountain or two, but I think La Grotta Ristorante Italiano has all it needs to claim success right now: two spirited proprietors and excellent authentic cuisine.

La Grotta is open for dinner, Monday through Saturday. Due to its size and popularity, reservations are essential. Jackets and ties are specified for gentlemen, and all major credit cards are welcomed. Prices are moderate.

TENDERLOIN OF VEAL WITH SHRIMPS

4 pieces veal tenderloin, 4 ounces (112 grams) each

salt and pepper, to taste

butter, to sauté

1 tablespoon (15 milliliters) chopped shallots

pinch of freshly crushed pepper

4 medium-sized shrimp

Pernod, to flame

1 cup (240 milliliters) cream

1/2 cup (120 milliliters) meat glaze

butter

finely chopped fresh basil

Season the meat with salt and pepper and sauté in butter until just undercooked. (Otherwise the meat becomes hard and dry.) In a saucepan, sauté the shallots, pepper, and shrimp, then flame with Pernod. Deglaze the pan with the cream, add the meat glaze, and simmer for a short while. Remove the pan from the heat and finish the sauce with butter. Pour the sauce over the veal and sprinkle with fresh basil.

Serves: 4

Wine: *Corvo white*

The Midnight Sun Restaurant presents its nationally known Scandinavian/Continental haute cuisine in strikingly modern surroundings at the Peachtree Center. In the center of this large restaurant is a glass enclosed, marble-tiered fountain. A strolling violin duo, playing nightly, adds to the Continental ambiance.

Elaborately prepared dishes are made with the lighter ingredients and sauces representative of the latest trends in cooking.

An unusual introduction to dinner is a thick, creamy, chilled apricot soup, punctuated with a topping of salmon caviar. This could be followed by Danish hors d'oeuvres.

À la carte dinner selections include salmon scallops with sorrel à la Troisgros (thin scallops of salmon sautéed and served with sorrel sauce, and fleuron) and pheasant and sweetbreads Rossini (breast of pheasant and braised sweetbreads with slices of Strasbourg goose liver, served with game sauce and grapes). For dessert, perhaps choose Baked Alaska Norwegian or Danish Aebleskiver.

There is a five-course, prix fixe dinner which includes everything from frogs legs Toscana to Queen Margrethe mousse, plus all the house wine you can drink. There is also an extensive list of imported and domestic wines in all price ranges.

The Midnight Sun is open for lunch Monday through Friday, and for dinner every night, and there is a Sunday Smorgasbrunch. Reservations are recommended. Jackets are requested, but ties are optional. Major credit cards are welcomed. Prices are medium to expensive.

Midnight Sun Restaurant

225 Peachtree Street
Atlanta, Georgia 30303
(404) 577-5050

Proprietor: Stig Jorgensen
Chef: Vagn Nielsen

SALMON TERRINE À LA THYKJAER

14 ounces (392 grams) sole fillet, julienne

7 ounces (196 grams) snapper, julienne

7 ounces (196 grams) salmon, julienne

7 ounces (196 grams) crabmeat, julienne

1 green pepper, diced

1 red pimento, diced

pinch of saffron

2 cups (480 milliliters) white wine

1 cup (240 milliliters) vermouth

2 teaspoons (10 milliliters) fish bouillon

1/2 ounce (15 milliliters) truffles

2 pounds (900 grams) salmon

1/2 teaspoon (2.5 milliliters) salt

2 eggs

1 quart (950 milliliters) whipping cream

2 teaspoons (10 milliliters) fish bouillon

2 teaspoons (10 milliliters) lobster base

unsalted pork fatback, sliced thinly, as needed

2 ounces (60 milliliters) gelatin

4 bay leaves

fresh thyme, to taste

Marinate the first 7 ingredients in the wine, vermouth, bouillon, and truffles for 12 hours.

Meanwhile, prepare the salmon mousse by chopping the 2 pounds (900 grams) of salmon in a food processor and slowly adding salt, eggs, whipping cream, fish bouillon, and lobster base.

Cover the bottom of a loaf pan that holds 1/2 gallon (1.9 liters) of liquid with thin slices of fatback and fill the pan with 2/3 of the mousse, leaving a hole in the center. Fill the center with the marinated mixture and cover with gelatin and the remaining mousse. Cover with fatback slices and top with bay leaves and thyme.

Wrap the entire pan in plastic film and aluminum foil to keep all air out. Bake in a 375° oven in a pan of water for 1 1/4 hours.

Remove the paper. Any water that has run off should be poured back into the pan at this time. Chill for 12 hours before serving.

Serves: 12

Wine: *White Burgundy, Chardonnay, or a dry Riesling*

Pano's & Paul's Restaurant

Proprietors:
Pano Karatassos and Paul Albrecht
Chef: Paul Albrecht

1232 West Paces Ferry Road, N.W.
Atlanta, Georgia 30327
(404) 261-3662

Pano's & Paul's Restaurant serves superior Continental cuisine in a subdued, romantic, turn-of-the-century atmosphere. The walls are covered with a paisley fabric, accented by brass wall sconces, paintings, mirrors, shirred fabrics, canopies and Victorian wooden side-pieces. Piano music drifts in from the bar. Quietly weaving in and out of the tables are very professional waiters dressed in traditional black waistcoats, bow ties, and long white aprons.

Every dinner begins with a basket of lahvosh, a crisp Armenian flat bread accompanied by a cheese spread composed of Roquefort, Parmesan and cream cheeses with herbs. Hot or cold appetizers include a flaky pastry filled with crabmeat, spinach, and feta cheese. There is also trout, which the restaurant smokes itself and serves with capers, slices of onion, and a horseradish sauce for dipping.

The house specialty is Les Supremes de Poularde en daube. For those who love tender veal, there is Les Medaillons de Veaux aux morilles Remy Martin (thick-cut medaillons of veal served in a sauce of cream, cognac, and morels). Other delicacies are the foie de veau sauté maison (calf's liver) and the coussin d'agneau (a grilled Madagascar lamb steak, served with a lively green peppercorn sauce).

The house dessert specialty is Mississippi Mudpie for two, a huge portion of coffee ice cream in a chocolate cookie crust with whipped cream and ground coffee beans. Also of interest are the chocolate mousse with strawberries and whipped cream, and the sabayon (egg whites blended with sugar, white wine and Kirschwasser, beaten to a foam and served chilled). There is a long list of European and California wines.

Pano's & Paul's is open for dinner only, Monday through Saturday. Reservations are advised, as is the wearing of jackets. Major credit cards are accepted. Prices are in the medium range.

LES SUPREMES DE POULARDE EN DAUBE

2 chicken breasts, halved, skinless and boneless

salt and pepper, to taste

flour, to dust

4 ounces (120 milliliters) clarified butter

2 ounces (56 grams) all-purpose flour

8 ounces (240 milliliters) chicken broth

2 ounces (60 milliliters) heavy cream

3 ounces (84 grams) precooked sweetbreads

2 ounces (56 grams) chanterelles

1 ounce (28 grams) walnut halves

1 ounce (30 milliliters) Calvados

8 ounces (224 grams) French puff pastry dough

1 egg, lightly beaten

Sprinkle the chicken breasts with salt and pepper. Dust very lightly with flour and sauté in clarified butter on both sides until a nice brown. Remove the chicken breasts and place them in a copper casserole with a lid.

Prepare a sauce by blending the all-purpose flour into the butter remaining in the skillet and sauté for 2-3 minutes on medium heat. Stir in the cold chicken broth and let simmer for approximately 8-10 minutes. Add heavy cream, salt, and pepper, and strain into a fine china cup.

Place the sweetbread morsels, chanterelles, and walnut halves into the casserole with the chicken breasts. Pour the sauce over all, then sprinkle on the Calvados and seal the casserole with 1/4-inch (.64-centimeter) thick puff pastry dough, approximately 2 1/2 inches (6.4 centimeters) wide around the edges of the lid. Decorate the sealing pastry with cut outs from dough scraps. Brush the dough with beaten egg and bake in a preheated oven at 375° for 12-14 minutes.

Cut away the pastry to free the lid. Serve the dish including some of the pastry.

Serves: 4

Wine: *Chateau Olivier*

Pittypat's Porch

Proprietor: A.J. Anthony
Chef: Bobby Hulata

25 International Boulevard, N.W.
Atlanta, Georgia
(404) 525-8228

Pittypat's Porch is the kind of restaurant you go to for fun, as well as for the very good southern cooking, which manages to reflect the influence of French, Spanish, English, and German cuisines. The key words here are "informal" and "relaxed". A rustic, southern decor features soft lighting, extensive use of red brick and mellow woods, copperware, pewterware, and wall-mounted specimens of wildlife such as boar, antelope, and buffalo. An organist plays popular southern melodies nightly.

Southern hospitality is expressed by Pittypat's Porch in an abundance of food, starting with a challenging 22-item "endless appetizer buffet" that is included with all entrées. The price of each entrée also includes a complete seven-course dinner. Steaks and fish are available, but the real specialties are roast pheasant, stuffed quail, venison, and their Country Captain (chicken served with noodles in a souvenir skillet you can take home). You might want to try the "Twelve Oaks Nibbler" (venison, buffalo, and veal with noodles), the "Tara" southern barbeque (back ribs, poultry leg, country ham, and

corn on the cob), or "Colonial Hunter" (a buffalo kebob with quail and a baked apple).

Specialty drinks are served in glasses that are yours for the taking, and of course, Pittypat's presents its interpretation of the traditional mint julep. There are also "Pittypat's Pitch" (a brew of vodka, passion juice, and "sacred herbs"), the "Scarlett" (their version of a frozen daquiri), and "Cotton Picker" (a blend of Georgia moonshine and scuppernong wine).

For an after-dinner treat, there is the Café Special. Made either with regular coffee or café espresso, the ingredients include Irish whiskey, Viennese brandy, and Dutch mint chocolate. There is a small list of imported and domestic wines.

This restaurant does cater to souvenir collectors, advising that all table items are for sale at the cashier's desk.

Pittypat's Porch serves dinner only, Monday through Saturday. Reservations are taken until 6 p.m. each night. Casual attire is suggested. All major credit cards are welcomed. Prices are moderate.

ROAST PHEASANT

1 2-3-pound (908-1362-gram)
pheasant

salt and pepper, to taste

1 bay leaf

1 clove garlic, crushed

few celery leaves

1 slice lemon

4 slices bacon

melted butter or margarine, as
needed

1 large onion, sliced

2 4-ounce (112-gram) cans
mushrooms

1 cup (240 milliliters) chicken broth
or 1 bouillon cube and water

Sprinkle the pheasant inside and out with salt
and pepper. Place the bay leaf, garlic, celery
leaves, and lemon in the cavity. Tie the legs
together with string. Turn the wings under.
Cover the breast with bacon slices and cheesecloth soaked in melted butter or margarine.
Place the pheasant, breast side up, in a baking
pan. Arrange the onion slices and mushrooms
with liquid around the pheasant. Pour chicken
broth over the bird. Roast at 350° for about 30
minutes per pound, or until tender, basting frequently with the liquid in the pan. Remove the
cheesecloth and string. Serve with its own
sauce.

Serves: 3-4

Wine: *Mouton Cadet*

Arnaud's serves gourmet French and Creole beef and seafood dishes at very reasonable prices in a dining room of unique beauty. The geometrically patterned mosaic tile floor creates an airy feeling, and the white linen cloths set on round and square tables add to the overall lightness of the room. Ceiling fans slowly turning overhead and white cast iron columns and standing plants also add to a pleasant ambiance. Arnaud's is a comfortable, friendly, yet classy place to dine.

Shrimp Arnaud is a peppery New Orleans-style appetizer, and they serve a variety of baked oysters, too. Oysters Suzette is the house specialty; it's prepared with bread crumbs, mushrooms, green peppers, and pimentos. The Shrimp Bisque Arnaud has a Creole tang.

Filet Mignon Charlemond is served with Béarnaise sauce. An unusual entrée is the Rock Cornish Game Hen Flambé Twelfth Night, and the Shrimp Creole and Crabmeat Monaco are two entrées that capture the characteristic savory New Orleans flavor. Arnaud's offers over a dozen vegetable preparations from a Potato Soufflé to Asparagus Hollandaise, Sautéed Cauliflower, and Ratatouille Creole. All the vegetables are fresh and aromatic. The Bread Pudding is a very special regional dessert which should be tried.

The wine list at Arnaud's is impressive, featuring imported and domestic selections in all price ranges. Mixed drinks are available, as well.

Arnaud's is open for dinner seven days a week and for lunch five days a week. Reservations are recommended, neat dress is a must, and all major credit cards are accepted. Prices are moderately expensive.

Arnaud's

813 Rue Bienville
New Orleans, Louisiana 70112
(504) 523-5433

Proprietor: Archie A. Casbarian

POMPANO EN CROÛTE

- **1 pound (454 grams) pastry dough**
- **4 inch x 4 inch (10 centimeter x 10 centimeter) fillet of pompano sliced thinly**
- **4 ounces (120 milliliters) Scallop Mousse (*recipe follows*)**
- **egg wash (1 egg yolk mixed with a small amount of water)**
- **Cream Fish Sauce (*recipe follows*)**

Divide the pastry dough into 4 sections. Roll the dough out very thin, about 1/4 inch (.6 centimeter). Put 2 ounces (56 grams) of fillet on one half of the rolled out dough. Top with 2 ounces (60 milliliters) of Scallop Mousse, cover with 1 ounce (28 grams) more of fillet. Brush the uncovered portion of the dough with egg wash. Fold the dough in half, covering the fillet and mousse, and seal the edges with your fingers. Cut the pastry shell into a fish shape and decorate with pieces of dough. Spread egg wash on top of the pastry shell and bake at 375° for 15-20 minutes until a light brown. Serve over Cream Fish Sauce.

Scallop Mousse

- **8 ounces (224 grams) scallops**
- **1/2 pint (240 milliliters) whipping cream**
- **3 egg yolks**
- **salt and pepper, to taste**
- **dash of cayenne pepper**
- **1/2 ounce (15 milliliters) French brandy**

To prepare Scallop Mousse: blend all ingredients together until the volume is almost double and consistency is smooth.

Cream Fish Sauce

- **pompano fish bones**
- **1/2 white onion**
- **1 bay leaf**
- **dash of leaf thyme**
- **5-6 whole black peppers**
- **1 slice skinned lemon**
- **1 clove garlic**
- **1/2 cup (120 milliliters) California Chablis**
- **water, as needed**
- **2 tablespoons (30 milliliters) butter**
- **2 tablespoons (30 milliliters) flour**
- **1 cup (240 milliliters) whipping cream**
- **dash of Angostura bitters**
- **dash of Tabasco sauce**
- **small amount of lemon juice**
- **salt and pepper, to taste**

To prepare Cream Fish Sauce: combine the first 8 ingredients and boil in enough water to cover for 15-20 minutes. Strain in a collander, then boil again and thicken with butter and flour. Vigorously whip to keep smooth and creamy. Boil slowly for another 10 minutes. Add whipping cream, strain again, then add the last 4 ingredients.

Wine: Chardonnay, Chateau St. Jean or Sterling Vineyard

Serves: 4

Brennan's

Proprietors:
Owen, Theodore, and James Brennan

417 Royal Street
New Orleans, Louisiana 70130
(504) 525-9713

Brennan's, housed in a pink stucco mansion with balconies and wrought iron railings, is very "New Orleans" in appearance and in its French Creole cooking. Under Brennan family ownership and direction, it has developed into a nationally recognized institution—the source of numerous innovations in cuisine and service, such as "Breakfast At Brennan's" and "Bananas Foster."

Southern hospitality is dispensed here on a grand scale. Over one thousand breakfasts and four hundred dinners are served on an average day.

Their special creation—"Breakfast At Brennan's"—is not to be missed when in New Orleans. Here is a breakfast menu with literally dozens of entrées illustrating the restaurant's adherence to Creole-influenced French haute cuisine. Anywhere else, it would constitute an excellent dinner menu, but at Brennan's—it's breakfast.

Wines and cocktails are available, along with hot soups, hors d'oeuvres, omelettes, meat and fish dishes, and desserts flambé. They serve as much wine and liquor on Sunday morning as on Saturday night.

Imagine a breakfast menu presenting oyster soup, Creole onion soup, ten omelettes, and other egg dishes such as their special Eggs Sardou (poached eggs atop creamed spinach and artichoke bottoms with Hollandaise sauce). Also included are ham steak, sirloin steak, escargots, pompano, sautéed baby veal topped with poached eggs and Hollandaise, trout, and quail in Burgundy sauce.

Dinner at Brennan's is more of the same. Creole seafood gumbo is a good introduction to a real New Orleans-style dinner. Other menu items include Oysters Brennan (baked with garlic butter sauce and Italian seasoned bread crumbs), Buster Crabs Béarnaise (soft shell crabs from Gulf waters sautéed in butter, then finished with Béarnaise sauce), Crepe Barbara (shrimp and lump crabmeat with lemon butter sauce in a crepe topped with Hollandaise and grated Parmesan cheese).

Breakfast, lunch, and dinner are served daily at Brennan's. Reservations are very necessary. Jackets are suggested for men at lunch, jackets and ties for dinner. The credit cards accepted are American Express, Visa, and Mastercharge. Prices are expensive.

SHRIMP CLEMENÇEAU

1/2 cup (120 milliliters) butter

3 pounds (1.35 kilograms) fresh shrimp, peeled and deveined

4 tablespoons (60 milliliters) garlic, finely minced

1 1/2 cups (360 milliliters) green onion, finely chopped

1 1/2 cups (360 milliliters) mushrooms, sliced

1 cup (240 milliliters) cooked green peas

4 teaspoons (20 milliliters) parsley, finely chopped

1 1/2 cups (360 milliliters) deep-fried diced potatoes

1/4 cup (60 milliliters) dry white wine

1 1/2 teaspoons (7.5 milliliters) salt, approximately

3/4 teaspoon (3.75 milliliters) pepper, approximately

Melt the butter in a large heavy skillet or sauté pan. Add the shrimp, garlic, green onion, and mushrooms. Sauté until lightly browned, stirring frequently but gently. Add the remaining ingredients and mix well. Cook for about 4-6 minutes longer. Serve on heated plates.

Serves: 8

Wine: *Pouilly Fumé or Muscadet*

Broussard's

819 Conti Street
New Orleans, Louisiana 70112
(504) 581-3866

Broussard's serves ample portions of charm and history along with its celebrated and traditional New Orleans Creole cuisine. Its charm and history are sensed when you first see the stuccoed terracotta front, a portico with a wrought-iron trellis border, and the flickering gas lamps. Inside, the main dining room (the Napoleon Room) is a blend of Burgundy tones and soft pastel pinks accented by a large Louis XVI mirror, empire sconces, and chandeliers. The smaller Provincial Room is done in Louis XVI style. The Napoleon Patio, with its ancient guava tree and lush greenery, leads you to the Victorian-style bar. Directly off the bar is the Sicilian Room featuring Sicilian artifacts.

Dinner can begin with Oysters Gresham (oysters in a white wine sauce with bread crumbs and Parmesan cheese) or a Broussard original, Shrimp Chandeleur. Several other oyster, shrimp, crab, and snail dishes are also offered.

The extensive menu features such à la carte entrées as Trout Conti (fresh, tender trout, poached and stuffed with shrimp and crabmeat, covered with sauce demi-Hollandaise and white wine with asparagus garni) and the Duck Nouvelle Orleans (roast duck served on a bed of rice, blended with oysters, mushrooms, fine herbs, and Creole orange sauce). Beef, veal, and lamb dishes are also very special.

Among the many entrées to choose from on the prix fixe dinner menu are Pompano Pontchartrain (fresh filet of pompano sautéed with baby soft shell crab covered with foamy butter and lemon), Chicken Clemenceau (spring chicken roasted and tossed with fresh mushrooms, green peas, shallots, demi-brabant potatoes and a touch of garlic), and Veal Gerard (baby white veal sautéed in butter and lemon, fine herbs with artichoke bottom and fresh mushrooms). The wine list offers many imported and domestic selections in all price ranges.

A perfect conclusion to a real New Orleans dinner is one of three flaming crepe offerings or the very rich Bananas Foster.

Broussard's is open every day for dinner only. Reservations are recommended. Men are required to wear jackets, and all major credit cards are welcomed. Prices are medium to expensive.

SHRIMP CHANDELEUR

4 ounces (120 milliliters) butter

4 green onions, cut finely

6 fresh mushrooms, sliced

2 slices Prosciutto ham, julienne

3 pounds (1.35 kilograms) raw deveined shrimp

1 quart (.95 liter) Heavy Cream Sauce (*recipe follows*)

1 tablespoon (15 milliliters) paprika

1/4 cup (60 milliliters) sherry wine

1 teaspoon (5 milliliters) chicken base

Melt the butter in a saucepan, add the green onions, mushrooms, and ham, and sauté at least 5 minutes over high heat. Add the shrimp and cook for 5 minutes. Blend the remaining ingredients in a saucepan and cook for 5 minutes. Serve in a casserole.

Heavy Cream Sauce

1 quart (.95 liter) milk

4 ounces (120 milliliters) butter

4 tablespoons (60 milliliters) flour

1 egg yolk

1 ounce (30 milliliters) sauterne

To prepare Heavy Cream Sauce: heat the milk over medium heat to scalding. Melt the butter in a separate saucepan over low heat, blend in the flour, and cook 3-4 minutes over low heat. Add the milk, bring to a boil, then simmer for 5 minutes. Beat the egg yolk with wine, then stir into the sauce.

Yields: 1 quart (.95 liter)

Wine: *Muscadet*

Serves: 6

Commander's Palace is located in the Garden District, a genteel and serene neighborhood that condenses much of the best of New Orleans on its tree-lined avenues and residential streets. The restaurant is housed in a large, wooden Victorian home constructed as a two-story restaurant-residence for Emile Commander in 1891. Today, the exterior is painted turquoise blue trimmed with white. The street-level dining room is walled in yellow and white linen. Light from outside streams through heavy window shutters and sparkles on the crystal prisms hanging from wall sconces and a magnificent Baccarat chandelier. The Garden Room features floor-to-ceiling windows, potted palms, and white iron chairs in the style of Chinese Chippendale. The incomparable Old South decor at Commander's Palace has charmed visitors for many years. The dining rooms have repeatedly been acknowledged as being among the country's most tastefully decorated.

And the menu? It is spectacular. The house specialties are Crabmeat Imperial, Stuffed Flounder, and Turtle Soup. They are prepared in the rich heritage of New Orleans and Creole cuisine. Even the weekend jazz brunches exude those flavors. Eggs Basin Street is a rice cake with red beans cooked with andouille. This combination is topped with a poached egg and Hollandaise sauce.

The wine list at Commander's Palace offers imported and domestic vintages in all price ranges; there is bar service as well.

Commander's Palace is open seven days a week, excepting only Christmas and Mardi Gras. Reservations are recommended, all major credit cards are honored, and jackets are required for gentlemen. Prices are moderately expensive.

Commander's Palace

1403 Washington Avenue
New Orleans, Louisiana 70130
(504) 899-8221

Proprietors:
Ella, Adelaide, Dick, and John Brennan

STUFFED FLOUNDER

3 tablespoons (45 milliliters) butter

1/4 cup (60 milliliters) finely chopped green onions

1/4 cup (60 milliliters) flour

3/4 cup (180 milliliters) fish or shrimp stock

3 tablespoons (45 milliliters) white wine

1/4 teaspoon (1.25 milliliters) salt

1/8 teaspoon (.6 milliliters) cayenne pepper

1 egg yolk, beaten

1/3 cup (80 milliliters) lump crabmeat, without shells

1/2 cup (120 milliliters) chopped, boiled, and peeled shrimp

1/2 dozen oysters, lightly blanched and chopped

2 teaspoons (10 milliliters) finely chopped parsley

4 1 1/2-pound (681-gram) flounders, head and bones removed

1 tablespoon (15 milliliters) paprika

1 1/2 tablespoons (22.5 milliliters) freshly grated Parmesan cheese

2 teaspoons (10 milliliters) bread crumbs

1/4 cup (60 milliliters) vegetable oil

To prepare the stuffing: melt the butter in a large skillet and sauté the green onions over medium heat until tender. Blend in the flour thoroughly. Reduce the heat to low and cook for 5 minutes, stirring constantly; do not brown. Remove from heat.

Blend in the fish stock, wine, salt, and pepper until smooth. Gradually add 1 cup (240 milliliters) of this mixture to the beaten egg yolk, stirring well to blend. Return all to the skillet and stir well. Return the pan to low heat and cook for 15 minutes, stirring constantly.

Add the crabmeat, shrimp, oysters, and parsley, mix well, heat thoroughly, then remove from heat.

To assemble: divide the stuffing among the flounders. Combine the paprika, Parmesan cheese, and bread crumbs and sprinkle over the stuffing. Close the stuffed fish with toothpicks or small skewers.

In a large heavy oven-proof skillet, sear the flounders on both sides over medium heat in the oil. Place the skillet in a preheated 400° oven for 10-15 minutes, or until the fish flakes easily. Suggestion: serve with lemon slices.

Serves: 4

Wine: *Chardonnay, Chateau St. Jean*

Galatoire's Restaurant

Proprietors: The Galatoire Family

209 Bourbon Street
New Orleans, Louisiana 70130
(504) 525-2021

Galatoire's Restaurant is not pretentious, but rather, it is a place where you can go to relax and enjoy French/Creole cooking in a real New Orleans atmosphere. Effective use is made of high ceilings, mirrors, fan lights, and bentwood chairs.

The dozens of items on the menu represent many of the most popular classic dishes on which New Orleans built its gastronomic reputation.

Appetizers named as house specialties include Shrimp Remoulade, Oysters Rockefeller, Oysters en Brochette, and Crabmeat Maison.

Trout Meunière Amandine is one of their most popular specialties on an entrée list which also offers Trout Marguery, Pompano Meunière Amandine, Crabmeat Yvonne, and Crabmeat Ravigote.

Poultry fanciers should consider the Chicken Clemenceau or the Chicken Firancière. For red meat lovers, there are first class Filet Béarnaise, Sirloin Marchand de Vin, or Lamb Chops Béarnaise—all Galatoire specialties.

Featured salads include Chef Salad Maison with Blue Cheese and Green Salad with Garlic. The wines (mostly French, with some German and California) may be chosen from a well-selected list. You are sure to find something to match whatever you are eating.

The dozen desserts on the menu include three with which Galatoire's has done something unusual: Coupe Princesse, Crepes Maison, or Café Brulot for two.

Galatoire's serves lunch and dinner Tuesday through Sunday. Reservations and credit cards are not accepted. Jackets and ties are a must for gentlemen. Prices are moderate.

TROUT MEUNIÈRE AMANDINE

salt and pepper, to taste

**4 6-8-ounce (168-224-gram) fillets
of speckled trout**

milk, as needed

flour, to dust

oil, for frying

1/2 pound (227 grams) butter

**4 ounces (112 grams) sliced, toasted
almonds**

juice of 1 lemon

**1/2 tablespoon (7.5 milliliters)
chopped parsley**

Salt and pepper the fillets. Dip the seasoned fillets in milk, then roll them in flour. Fry the fish in hot oil in a shallow pan until they are golden on both sides.

In a separate pan, melt and continuously whip the butter until it is brown and frothy. Add the sliced almonds and lemon juice. Pour this sauce over the trout. Garnish with chopped parsley and serve.

Serves: 4

the

To my mind, New Orleans' **Versailles Restaurant** represents an enduring tribute to classic French grandeur. Located in the heart of the city's Garden District, this establishment, with its luxuriously decorated three main dining salons and bar area, is intended to reflect the elegance of the Palace of Versailles in France during the reign of Louis XIV. Thanks to the decorating ability of co-manager Evelyn Preuss, it works.

Evelyn's partner is her husband, Chef Gunter Preuss, who matches his wife's creation of quiet elegant dining with a magnificent array of classic French recipes—including Escargots Bourguignon en croûte, Mignonette de Boeuf au Moelle, and, for dessert, an unusual Lemon Tequilla Soufflé.

Chef Preuss, who was formally trained in England, France, Germany, Switzerland, and Sweden, claims his specialty is Bouillabaisse Marseillance, but I suggest to you that there are quite a few other specialties on the Versailles Restaurant's menu.

In addition to the charming atmosphere and fine food, the restaurant has an impressive list of imported and domestic wines in all price ranges and features California vintages as its house wines.

The Versailles serves dinner only, 5:30-7:30 p.m. Monday through Saturday. Seating is only 160, so call for reservations. The dress code requests jackets for men, no jeans. All major credit cards are accepted. Prices are moderately expensive.

Versailles Restaurant

2100 St. Charles Avenue
New Orleans, Louisiana 70130
(504) 524-2535

Proprietor/Chef: Gunter Preuss

LEMON TEQUILLA SOUFFLÉ

2/3 cup (160 milliliters) sugar

1 cup (240 milliliters) water

6 egg yolks

3 ounces (90 milliliters) white wine

2 1/2 ounces (75 milliliters) lemon juice

1 1/2 ounces (45 milliliters) tequilla

1 1/2 cups (360 milliliters) whipped cream

6 lemon halves, hollowed out

whipped cream and 6 mint leaves, to garnish

Combine the sugar with water in a saucepan and boil gently until the mixture begins to thicken (syrup stage). Remove from heat and let cool thoroughly. When the mixture is cold, combine it with the egg yolks, wine, lemon juice, and tequilla.

Cook this mixture over a low flame, whisking constantly until the foam goes down. (Taste to be sure the eggs are cooked.) Then place in the refrigerator and stir occasionally to cool. When cool, fold in the whipped cream and place in the freezer.

To assemble: place the soufflé in hollowed out lemons, put on a bed of shaved ice, and freeze. Just before serving, garnish with whipped cream from a tube and place a mint leaf on each lemon half.

Serves: 6

Perdita's

Proprietors:
The Gordon Bennett Family
Chef: J.L. Lemmon

10 Exchange Street
Charleston, South Carolina 29401
(803) 577-4364

The building in which **Perdita's** Restaurant is located was built in the mid-1700s. "Perdita" is the name of a leading role in Shakespeare's *Winter's Tale* which, in the late 1700s, was played by Mrs. Paul Robinson, a major British personality of the era. Legend has it that she visited Charleston on tour and was the cause of a duel between a Southerner and a New Englander.

Today, near the spot where the duel occurred, you enter Perdita's through a black oak door. The main dining room is graced by brick arches and red leather latticed back chairs and beautifully appointed wall sconces. A raised and balustraded smaller dining room has a cameo carved on the back of each chair. Their third room is modeled after the Brooks Club of London; it features velvet flocked walls, antique paintings, and Queen Anne chairs.

The menu at Perdita's offers a wide variety of classic preparations, and the cooking has been officially acclaimed—time and again. Although there are fine beef, lamb, chicken, and game dishes, seafood is the specialty of the house. Shrimp, crab, and oyster appetizers are served hot and cold. The soup list includes shrimp bisque and Charleston She Crab Soup. Main course specialties are the Lobster Dainties Dupree, and "Fruits de Mer" — a magnificent broiled seafood combination. There are also Chateaubriand in Sauce Espagnole, Double Cut Lamb Chops, and Brace of Native Quail with Pâté de Fois Gras. The wine list is modest but of excellent quality, and cocktails are served.

Perdita's is open for dinner six days a week. Make reservations and dress neatly. All major credit cards are honored. Prices are moderately expensive.

CHARLESTON SHE CRAB SOUP

2 quarts (1.9 liters) milk

1 small onion, finely chopped

4 ounces (112 grams) white crabmeat

1/8 pound (56 grams) butter

1/4 tablespoon (3.75 milliliters) paprika

1/8 teaspoon (.6 milliliters) Ac'cent

2 ounces (56 grams) crab roe

flour and water, optional

salt and pepper, to taste

dash of paprika and finely diced parsley, to garnish

dry sherry, as needed

Put milk in a double boiler and bring to the boiling point.

While milk is heating, sauté the onion and crabmeat in butter along with paprika and Ac'cent. Crumble the crab roe into the pan and saute for 1-2 minutes longer. Add these ingredients to the heated milk and bring back almost to the boiling point. (If soup needs to be thickened, add flour and water mixture.) Salt and pepper to taste. Keep over low heat for 25-30 minutes.

To serve: garnish with dash of paprika and diced parsley. After serving, add a splash of dry sherry to each cup.

Yields: 2 1/2 quarts (2.4 liters)

Wine: *Johannesburg Riesling, Napa Valley*

Sciara's Palazzino is a casual, family-style Italian restaurant owned and managed by master chef Sam Sciara, his son Pete, as host, and their families. Much of the food at Palazzino is homemade, with the cheeses, salami, and some pasta imported from Italy. Many of the recipes used have been in the Sciara family for generations and make liberal use of imported Italian wines and spices.

You would do well to start off with their appetizer specialty Fettucine Sciara. Prepared tableside, this is made with a touch of garlic, Parmesan cheese, cream and parsley.

Cannelloni Béchamel, a much-favored entrée, consists of chicken and veal wrapped in crepes topped with a white cheese sauce. Another specialty is Lasagna Salvatore — stuffed with fresh mushrooms, Ricotta

cheese, almonds, chicken, ham, Italian sausage, spices, and covered with meat sauce.

Veal Piccata (in which slices of milkfed veal are sautéed in a white wine and lemon butter sauce, then served with spaghetti sautéed in garlic butter sauce) leads the many veal favorites that also includes Stuffed Veal Supreme (a 14 oz. veal chop stuffed with cheese, Prosciutto ham and Italian bread crumbs, sautéed in Madeira wine sauce, and served with spaghetti and garlic butter sauce).

Traditional, but exceptionally prepared Italian desserts end a fine meal. Palazzino serves dinner every day. Reservations are advised for weekdays only. Dress should be casual to match the atmosphere. Major credit cards are accepted. Prices are moderate.

Sciara's Palazzino

6155 Poplar
Memphis, Tennessee 38119
(901) 767-9541

Proprietor: Pete S. Sciara
Chef: Sam J. Sciara

VEAL PICCATA WITH LINGUINI

2 pounds (908 grams) veal, sliced thinly, cut in 2-inch (5-centimeter) squares

1 cup (240 milliliters) all-purpose flour

1/2 cup (120 milliliters) butter

1 cup (240 milliliters) white wine

juice from 2 fresh lemons

salt and pepper, to taste

linguini with Garlic-Butter Cream Sauce (*recipe follows*)

Sprinkle the veal with flour and sauté in butter. Slowly add wine, then lemon juice. Sprinkle with a little salt and pepper. Turn once or twice while cooking. Put veal on a hot plate. Add linguini to the side of the plate and cover with Garlic-Butter Cream Sauce.

Garlic-Butter Cream Sauce

1/4 pound (113 grams) butter

1 clove garlic, chopped finely

1 tablespoon (15 milliliters) chopped parsley

1 cup (240 milliliters) all-purpose flour

1 teaspoon (5 milliliters) Ac'cent

1 cup (240 milliliters) white wine

juice of 1 fresh lemon

1 quart (.95 liter) milk

Melt the butter. Add the garlic and sauté until a light brown. Stir in the parsley, flour, and Ac'cent. Add the wine and lemon juice. Slowly, stir in the milk, taking care not to add it too fast or get it too hot or the sauce will curdle. Serve the sauce over linguini as a side dish for veal piccata or freeze the sauce for later use.

Serves: 8

The ambiance of **Patry's French Restaurant** is warm, friendly, and very pleasant with fresh flowers on the tables, soft lighting, and French music in the background.

There are two specialties in which the Patry family takes particular pride: their own versions of Le Carre D'Agneau Persille pour deux (a tender roast rack of lamb with broiled tomatoes for two); and Le Chateaubriand en Papillote pour deux. Other meat dishes include Le Bifteck au Poivre Flambé au Cognac (flaming peppered steak with cognac, served with Patry's special sauce) and L'Escalope de Veau Piscatta ou à la crème (veal with lemon butter and capers or with cream sauce and mushrooms).

The seafood selections include Les Filet de Dover Sole Grenoblaise ou Meunière (filet of Dover sole with lemon butter and capers), Les Grenouilles à la crème ou Provençale (frogs legs in cream sauce or sauté in garlic butter sauce), Scallops Meunière ou Proven-çale (scallops with lemon butter sauce or garlic butter), Les Crevettes Portugaise (shrimp sauté in garlic butter and tomatoes). These are essentially simple, basic dishes that, when done well, are the essence of great French cuisine.

If you dine as the French do, you would choose a salad such as L'Endive, La Caesar Salad pour deux, or Les Coeurs de Palmiers vinaigrette (hearts of palm) to come after your entrée.

Flaming desserts such as Les Cherry Jubilee, Les Bananas Foster, and Les Crepes Suzette are all fun for the show as well as the taste.

Patry's is open for dinner every night but Monday. Reservations are recommended. Proper attire is required, which means jackets and ties for gentlemen. Major credit cards are honored. Prices are moderately expensive.

Patry's
French Restaurant

2504 McKinney Avenue
Dallas, Texas 75221
(214) 748-3754

Proprietor/Chef: George Patry

CRABMEAT IN PAPRIKA SAUCE

2 tablespoons (30 milliliters) finely
chopped shallots

6 tablespoons (90 milliliters) butter

1 cup (240 milliliters) dry white wine

2 teaspoons (10 milliliters) Spanish
paprika

2 tablespoons (30 milliliters)
all-purpose flour

2 cups (480 milliliters) milk

1/4 cup (60 milliliters) whipping cream

12 ounces (336 grams) Alaskan king
crab

4-8 fresh mushrooms, sliced

chopped parsley, to garnish

Sauté the shallots in 1/3 of the butter until a golden brown. They should be the color of hazelnuts when done. Stir in the wine and paprika; slowly bring to a boil. Remove from heat and set aside.

Melt the remaining butter in a saucepan. Stir in the flour; cook, stirring constantly, for 5 minutes. Add the milk; cook until smooth and thickened. Stir in the shallot mixture and bring to a boil. Add the whipping cream gradually, stirring constantly. As soon as the cream is mixed in, remove from heat immediately.

Divide the crabmeat into 4 individual casseroles or scallop shells. Divide the mushrooms equally among the dishes over the crabmeat. Pour the sauce over all. Bake at 400° for 5-7 minutes, then garnish with chopped parsley and serve.

Serves: 4

Wine: *Puligny Montrachet*

Brennan's of Houston

Proprietor: Noel Hennebery

3300 Smith Street
Houston, Texas 77006
(713) 522-9711

Brennan's of Houston is a direct descendant of the internationally famous Brennan's of New Orleans. It too carries on the rich tradition of Creole and French cooking. You feel the New Orleans influence, even in the breakfast preparations. Fried beans, seasoned rice, and tomato-based sauces (along with a Bloody Mary, perhaps) are touches that constitute unusual twists to the morning meal basics of eggs and meats.

The dinner menu is equally interesting. Trout Kottwitz is sautéed with artichoke hearts and mushrooms and topped with lemon sauce. Filet Mignon Debris is a crispy outside, tender inside filet topped with crumbles of roast beef that have been simmered in a rich cognac stock. The entire preparation is then covered with a tangy haute creole sauce. For dessert, a Brennan's specialty is Sour Cream Crepes. They are filled with crushed strawberries and flamed in liqueur.

The Brennan's wine cellar boasts a large selection of French, California, and German wines in all price ranges.

Proprietor Hennebery's experience includes service in London, New York, and Boston. He's been with Brennan's of Houston for 13 years, and he is as proud of his establishment's ambiance as he is of its food.

The softly-lit, comfortable, fabric-lined dining room overlooks a flowered patio. There's a cocktail lounge for pre-meal socializing, and at Brennan's there's always a lot of friendly mixing.

The restaurant is open daily for breakfast, lunch, and dinner. Call ahead for reservations and dress formally. All credit cards are honored and prices are expensive.

BANANAS FOSTER

2 1/2 cups (360 milliliters) brown sugar

1 tablespoon (15 milliliters) cinnamon

1 cup (240 milliliters) butter

4 ounces (120 milliliters) banana liqueur

8 ripe bananas, peeled and sliced lengthwise

4 ounces (120 milliliters) white rum

8 large scoops of vanilla ice cream

Melt the brown sugar, cinnamon, and butter in a flat cooking pan, then add the banana liqueur and the sliced bananas. Baste the bananas with the hot liquid until well saturated with the liquid. Add the rum and allow to flame. Continue basting until the flame burns out. Serve immediately over the ice cream in individual dishes.

Serves: 8

Wine: *Chandon California Champagne*

Kaphan's Restaurant

Proprietor: Peter Tomac

7900 South Main Street
Houston, Texas
(713) 668-0491

Kaphan's Restaurant caters to fans of fine American and French cuisine and to football and baseball fans, too. Presumably, many of them are the same. There is a display of autographed All-Star souvenir programs, baseballs signed by Babe Ruth in 1927, 1928, 1929, autographed National League baseballs from 1952 to the present, National and American League bats autographed by all players, and an autographed collection of National Football League balls from recent years.

The wine list covers the major wine producing areas of the world, with imported and domestic selections in all price ranges.

Appetizers include Texas Gulf Shrimp Cocktail Supreme, Crab Claws, Crab or Oyster Bisque, or Kaphan's Creole Gumbo with Rice.

A popular house specialty is the Seafood Platter—a blend of fried tenderloin of trout, stuffed crab, fried shrimp, deviled crab claw, fried oyster, shrimp salad, and fried scallops. Another specialty bears the unusual title of a

"Dichotomy of Oysters, Something Very Special" on piping hot rock salt—offering two each of Oysters Rockefeller, Buccaneer, Bienville, and Casino. The management advises that, because of the ascending flavors, they should be eaten counterclockwise.

Another unusual specialty is Fish Throats— Gulf fish throats fried or broiled to taste. Equally interesting is Filet of Redfish Steak Ponchartrain—filet of redfish sautéed in brown butter, topped with fresh crabmeat and shrimp in a white, creamy wine sauce.

Char-broiled dishes include Noisette of Beef, which is sautéed in sweet cream butter, seasonings, with Burgundy sauce and mushrooms en casserole on toast points. There are also hearty portions of prime sirloin, filet mignon, rib eye steak, and fried or broiled chicken.

Kaphan's is open for lunch and dinner every day but Wednesday. Reservations are advised. Casual attire prevails, and all major credit cards are welcomed. Prices are in the medium range.

OYSTERS BROILED IN SHERRY WINE SAUCE

salt and pepper, to taste

24 oysters

flour, to dredge

butter or cooking oil, to grill

1/4 cup (60 milliliters) fresh lemon juice

1 cup (240 milliliters) A1 sauce, or as needed

2 tablespoons (30 milliliters) Lea & Perrins Worcestershire sauce

2 ounces (60 milliliters) pale dry sherry wine, or as needed

2 tablespoons (30 milliliters) flour

3 tablespoons (45 milliliters) water

Salt and pepper the oysters, then dredge them in flour and grill them on a lightly buttered griddle on top of the stove until crisp and browned on both sides. *Do not broil in oven.* (If no griddle is available, use a heavy skillet on top of the stove.) Sprinkle the oysters with butter or cooking oil on both sides while grilling.

To prepare Sherry Wine Sauce: heat the lemon juice, A1 Sauce, Worcestershire sauce, and sherry in a saucepan over low heat, but do not allow to come to a boil. Blend the flour and water into the thoroughly heated sauce to thicken it. Correct the seasoning to taste. Add A1 Sauce if too thin, or sherry if too thick and highly seasoned.

Place the freshly grilled oysters on a hot serving plate and dress with the heated sauce. Insert frilled toothpicks in the oysters. The sauce can be saved, strained, re-heated and used again.

Serves: 4 as appetizer

Wine: *Chablis or Pinot Chardonnay*

Tony's features the cuisine of France as well as Mediterranean dishes and the light, subtle refinements of northern Italian cooking. The governing principle is a blend of classical haute cuisine and contemporary *nouvelle cuisine.*

The ambiance is quiet with an understated splendor. Blacktie European service prevails in each of the three dining rooms, which include a wine cellar for private dining only. There are banks of fresh flowers, fresh flowers on every table, original modern paintings, and antique Chinese porcelains. In the main dining room hangs a priceless, strikingly beautiful 26-foot Chinese screen, circa 1690.

Tony's wine cellar shelters a collection of 140,000 bottles representing more than 300 different wines, cognacs, and ports.

Food literally fit for a king may be sampled in appetizers such as Petite Omelette Beluga, Crepe Contessa, and an incredible Fettuccine à la Portanova prepared with caviar. A selection of soups includes an outstanding Bisque d'Homard and French Onion Gratinée.

Some of the entrée specialties are Whole Roast Duckling with wild rice for two, Individual Whole Poached Trout Véronique or Fines Herbes for two, and Rack of Lamb Persilee for two. Capon is served five ways, and there are seven veal dishes starring Côte de Veau aux Morilles and Escalope de Veau Rossini. The beef dishes are equally notable.

A simple end to the meal is often the best—fruit and cheese—but if your taste runs to the more elaborate, you will be attracted to the Soufflés Grand Marnier or au Chocolat, or perhaps Bananas Flambé.

Tony's serves luncheon Monday through Friday; dinner, Monday through Saturday. Reservations are certainly needed. Jackets and ties are required. Major credit cards are honored. Prices are expensive.

Tony's

1801 South Post Oak
Houston, Texas 77056
(713) 622-6778

Proprietor: Tony Vallone

STRAWBERRY-RASPBERRY SOUFFLÉ

2 cups (480 milliliters) sliced ripe
strawberries

sugar, as needed

2 tablespoons (30 milliliters) red
currant jelly

3 tablespoons (45 milliliters) butter

3 tablespoons (45 milliliters) flour

1/2 cup (120 milliliters) milk

4 egg yolks, beaten

1 cup (240 milliliters) raspberry
purée, fresh or frozen

5 egg whites

1/2 teaspoon (2.5 milliliters) cream of
tartar

Place the strawberries in a dish and sprinkle them with a little sugar. Beat the currant jelly with a fork and pour it over the sweetened strawberries.

In the top part of a double boiler, over boiling water, melt the butter and stir in the flour. Cook for a few minutes, then stir in the milk. Cook for about 5 minutes, stirring constantly, until all is blended into a smooth sauce. Remove the top part of the double boiler from heat and allow to cool for a while. Then add the beaten egg yolks. Stir until the mixture is smooth. Add the puréed raspberries, sweeten with 1 tablespoon (15 milliliters) sugar, if necessary, and set aside to cool for about 15 minutes.

Beat the egg whites. Sprinkle in the cream of tartar while beating. Combine vigorously. Then, dribble the cooled raspberry purée mixture over the whites. Lift and fold carefully until all is gently blended.

Heat the sliced strawberries and place them in the bottom of a buttered and sugared 2-quart (1.9-liter) soufflé dish. Pour the raspberry-egg white mixture over them. Bake in a preheated 350° oven for about 25 minutes. Test for doneness before removing from the oven and serving.

Serves: 4-6

Central Region

illinois

indiana

michigan

minnesota

missouri

ohio

wisconsin

the Cottage

Proprietors:
Gerald and Carolyn Buster

525 Torrence Avenue
Calumet City, Illinois 60409
(312) 891-3900

The Cottage is a small, free-standing, typically French country inn that the Busters built and decorated right in Calumet City.

The menu is chalked on blackboards conveniently hung around the room. The fare, which is influenced by the seasons and the availability of first-rate ingredients, is sophisticated European, with emphasis on country French. Everything is made fresh from the start on the premises and to order.

You can begin dinner with a selection from a small, well-chosen wine list containing some of the better French vintage years. Then a Country Pâté en croûte (veal, pork and beef baked in a flaky pastry crust and served with a mustard sauce) or maybe the Ballontine of Veal (studded with pistachio nuts and green peppercorns, then topped with a light orange sauce). The soups, especially the cream soups, are something special—fresh and homemade.

Cottage Schnitzel is the chef's special entrée. A fresh fish favorite is a firm, meaty, double-sauced Rosemary Grouper—drenched in butter and cognac sauce, scented with rosemary, and followed by a superb Louis sauce.

Steak Viennoise is a tenderloin, soaked in a mustard coating, then sautéed to a crisp exterior and topped by twice-fried onion sauce made from the pan drippings and Roquefort cheese. A crisp Roast Duckling has a light, fruity, not-too-sweet cherry or plum sauce. Other entrées include pork and lamb dishes.

Desserts include Chocolate Surprise (a tall chocolate torte stuffed with a rich chocolate mousse, with a chocolate glaze, topped with a mound of whipped cream), Floating Island, Raspberry Gateau, Baked Alaska with fruit sauce, Schwarzwalder Kirschtorte, and a homemade Apple Strudel like none other you have ever tasted.

The Cottage is open Tuesday through Saturday for dinner only. Reservations are recommended. Gentlemen should wear jackets. Visa and Mastercard are honored. Prices range from medium to expensive.

"THE COTTAGE" SCHNITZEL

2 large eggs

2 tablespoons (30 milliliters) flour

2 tablespoons (30 milliliters) freshly grated Parmesan cheese

1/2 cup (120 milliliters) milk

    salt, white pepper, nutmeg, and freshly chopped parsley, to taste

2 pounds (908 grams) pork tenderloin, trimmed

    flour, to dust

    butter, to sauté

    freshly squeezed lemon juice, as needed

To prepare batter: place eggs, flour, Parmesan cheese, milk, and seasonings in a blender container and blend together at high speed for 2 minutes.

Slice the pork tenderloin and pound each slice into an approximate 3-inch (8-centimeter) thin medallion. Dip each medallion first in flour, then place in batter.

Melt enough butter to cover the bottom of a heavy frying pan. Quickly sauté the medallions in the butter until browned on each side. Remove to a serving tray and quickly deglaze the frying pan with lemon juice. Pour the pan juices over the pork medallions and serve immediately.

Serves: 4-6

Wine: *German Spatlese*

Chicago was once the meat packing capital of the world and the **Blackhawk Restaurant** on North Wabash Avenue extends the city's tradition by serving incomparably flavorful and tender prime beef.

The Blackhawk is sixty years old and was opened by proprietor Don Roth's father, Otto Roth. Don joined the staff, after receiving his Bachelor's degree from the University of Illinois, and went on to turn the Blackhawk into the landmark of downtown Chicago it is today.

This restaurant also enjoys a reputation for serving the finest prime rib available anywhere. The open hearth broiled prime steaks—two sizes of each cut are offered—are nearly as popular as the prime rib. The fresh Boston Scrod, flown in from the Atlantic and served with a bread crumb sauce, is a special treat for midwestern diners. The Blackhawk's wine list is modest but selected for quality. There's a busy cocktail lounge, and the dining room rotates art exhibits. The restaurant offers a complimentary shuttle service to nearby theaters and hotels.

Blackhawk Restaurant is open for lunch and dinner six days a week and for dinner only on Sunday. Neat dress is a must, reservations are suggested, and all major credit cards are honored. Prices are moderately expensive.

Blackhawk Restaurant

139 North Wabash Avenue
Chicago, Illinois 60602
(312) 726-0100

Proprietor: Don Roth

BLACKHAWK SPINNING SALAD BOWL

3 ounces (84 grams) cream cheese, softened

3 ounces (84 grams) blue cheese, crumbled

5 - 6 tablespoons (75 - 90 milliliters) water

1 egg

1 tablespoon plus 1 1/2 teaspoons (22.5 milliliters) lemon juice

1 cup (240 milliliters) vegetable oil

1/4 cup (60 milliliters) red wine vinegar

1/4 teaspoon (1.25 milliliters) sharp prepared mustard

3/4 teaspoon (3.75 milliliters) paprika

3/4 teaspoon (3.75 milliliters) salt

1/4 teaspoon (1.25 milliliters) garlic powder

1/4 teaspoon (1.25 milliliters) white pepper

1 tablespoon (15 milliliters) sugar

2 tablespoons (30 milliliters) snipped chives

1 1/2 teaspoons (7.5 milliliters) Worcestershire sauce

2 tablespoons (30 milliliters) salad and sandwich sauce

8 cups (1.92 liters) bite-size pieces salad greens: Bibb lettuce, iceberg lettuce, and endive

seasoned salt, to taste

1 hard-cooked egg, chopped

freshly ground pepper, to taste

8 anchovy fillets

To prepare the cheese mixture: beat the cheeses until smooth. Beat in water, 1 tablespoon (15 milliliters) at a time, until mixture is of pouring consistency.

Place the egg, lemon juice, and 1/4 of the oil in a blender and blend on medium speed for 15 seconds. Increase to high speed and add the remaining oil very slowly. Turn off the blender occasionally and clean the sides of the container with a rubber spatula.

Add the vinegar, mustard, seasonings, sugar, chives, Worcestershire sauce and salad sauce to the blender, cover, and blend on high speed until smooth.

Place the salad greens in a bowl. Pour enough dressing over the greens to coat. Sprinkle the salad with seasoned salt and chopped egg. Toss gently 3 times. Sprinkle with pepper. Add 2-3 tablespoons (30-45 milliliters) of the reserved cheese mixture. Toss gently 3 times. Garnish with anchovies and serve.

Remaining dressing and cheese mixture can be stored covered in a refrigerator for up to 2 weeks.

Serves: 4-6

the Cape Cod Room

Proprietor: The Drake Hotel
Chef: K. Bud Okubo

The Drake Hotel
140 East Walton Street
Chicago, Illinois 60611
(312) 787-2200

The Cape Cod Room in the Drake Hotel is a complete fish restaurant with every kind of the freshest seafood served in dozens of unique ways. Three thousand pounds are flown in each week from Massachusetts, Maryland, and Florida for inspection and approval by keen-eyed Executive Chef K. Bud Okubo, who has been with the Drake for 30 years.

The Cape Cod Room is quaint and colorful, with the intimacy of an old-fashioned seafarer's inn. Seascape murals and dark wood paneling form the backdrop for rugged captains' tables draped with red checkered tablecloths, polished copper pots and chowder kettles, huge green bottles, floats, lobster traps, wall-mounted prize specimens from the sea, and an antique pot-bellied stove.

There are several fine soups offered. If you are willing to wait the half hour needed to prepare it, you will be amply rewarded with the Bouillabaisse Marseillaise. It is composed of a variety of fresh and saltwater fishes and seafoods with fresh vegetable garniture, seasoned with garlic, parsley, thyme, saffron, and Chablis wine and served with garlic French bread.

Numerous fish, oyster, crab, lobster, scallop, and shrimp dishes are served sautéed, broiled, poached, or steamed to order. The extensive à la carte menu presents nine ways to enjoy oysters, five seafood stews, three sole dishes, in addition to French turbot, salmon, Colorado rainbow trout, six bay scallop dishes, five crabmeat dishes, seven variations on shrimp, and Maine lobster served eight ways. One of the most popular of these is Chef Okubo's Pompano-Papillote.

A full selection of imported and domestic wines is also available.

A separate oyster bar concentrates on serving clam and oyster stews, soups, sandwiches, and platters of fresh, raw shellfish in season.

The Cape Cod Room is open daily for lunch and dinner. Reservations are advised, particularly on weekends. Gentlemen are requested to wear jackets. Major credit cards are welcomed. Prices are moderate to medium.

POMPANO-PAPILLOTE À LA DRAKE

1 cup (240 milliliters) sliced fresh mushrooms

1 tablespoon (15 milliliters) chopped shallots

2 tablespoons (30 milliliters) butter

3/4 cup (180 milliliters) dry red wine

3/4 cup (180 milliliters) water

1/2 teaspoon (2.5 milliliters) Worcestershire sauce

6 7-ounce (196-gram) pompano fillets

1 tablespoon (15 milliliters) all-purpose flour

2 tablespoons (30 milliliters) cold water

1 5-ounce (140-gram) can lobster, drained and diced

oiled parchment paper

In a 12-inch (30.5-centimeter) skillet, cook the mushrooms and shallots in butter. Stir in the wine, 3/4 cup (180 milliliters) water, salt, and Worcestershire sauce. Add the fish fillets. Bring to a boil, reduce the heat, and cover and simmer for 4-5 minutes or just until the fish is done. Remove the fish.

Boil the pan liquid hard until reduced to 3/4 cup (180 milliliters). Blend the flour and remaining water and stir into the reduced liquid in the skillet. Cook and stir until thickened and bubbly. Stir in the lobster.

Cut 6 large valentine hearts from parchment paper, about 18 x 14 inches (46 x 36 centimeters). Brush the top side with oil. Place one fish fillet on the left half of each heart; top with some of the lobster sauce. Fold the right half of the paper heart over the fillet, turning all edges to form a tight seal. Bake in a 350° oven for 10-15 minutes until bags begin to puff.

Serve on a china platter, allowing each person to open a bag.

Serves: 6

Wine: *Pinot Chardonnay, Simi*

Cricket's, Ltd. can perhaps be best described as "slick", and I mean that very complimentarily. Everything about this establishment is efficient and exemplary—and it is so without being futuristic and plastic. On the contrary, this restaurant is very warm—warm decor with checkered tablecloths, crystal and silver tableware, beamed ceilings, and red leather—warm service with captains and waiters pleasantly and efficiently attending to your every need.

The force behind the successful demeanor of Cricket's is Alan Ireland, the general manager and a real professional hotel/restaurant man. Among the force in the kitchen is Chef Guy Petit, whose credentials include prior stints with such great establishments as Maxim's and the Plaza Athenee in Paris. The house specialty, Veal Cricket, is his creation. Chef Petit and his staff are consistent in maintaining the high quality of Cricket's standards—reliable service and excellent Continental food such as superb Crème Senéglaise, Sweetbreads Sauté, à L'Estragon, and Strawberries Romanoff.

The restaurant, which is located in the Tremont Hotel, is open for lunch and dinner, seven days a week. Seating is only 102, so reservations are a must. Ties and jackets are required for men, no slacks for ladies. All major credit cards are accepted. Prices are moderately expensive.

Cricket's, Ltd.

100 East Chestnut Street
Tremont Hotel
Chicago, Illinois 60611
(312) 280-2100

General Manager: Alan Ireland
Chef: Guy R. Petit

VEAL CRICKET

2 3-ounce (84-gram) veal escalopines

clarified butter, to sauté

1 tablespoon (15 milliliters)
mushroom purée

1/2 cup (120 milliliters) Mornay Sauce
(*recipe follows*)

2 tablespoons (30 milliliters)
demi-glaze sauce, prepared

watercress, to garnish

Sauté the veal lightly in clarified butter for 2 minutes on each side. Place escalopines on dinner plates, spread mushroom purée over the veal. Top with Mornay Sauce and brown under the broiler. Add the demi-glaze sauce around the edges and garnish with watercress. Serve.

Mornay Sauce

1/4 cup (60 milliliters) butter

1/2 cup (120 milliliters) flour

3 cups (720 milliliters) boiling milk

1/2 cup (120 milliliters) shredded
Swiss cheese

salt and pepper, to taste

2 egg yolks

Melt the butter and add flour to it. Slowly pour this mixture over the boiling milk and let simmer for 5 minutes. Add Swiss cheese, salt, and pepper. Remove from heat and add the egg yolks. If sauce is too thick, add some cold milk to it.

Yields: approximately six 1/2-cup (120-milliliter) servings

Wine: *Chambertin, Louis Latour, 1971*

Serves: 1

Maxim's de Paris

Proprietor: Nancy F. Goldberg

1300 Astor Street
Chicago, Illinois 60610
(312) 943-1111

Maxim's de Paris, located in Chicago, serves the same classical French cuisine as its famed namesake in Paris. This Maxim's decor and ambiance is a frank, faithful reproduction of the original. The atmosphere is soft, subdued, and romantic, with art nouveau decor, pink shaded table lamps, mirrors, and red velvet covered walls. In such a setting, you cannot help but dine leisurely and with attention paid equally to your food and your guest.

The wine list here emphasizes many of the more notable estate-bottled vintages, along with American and German wines. Prices run from moderate to expensive.

Cold hors d'oeuvres include foie gras truffe, smoked Norwegian or Scotch salmon, and Maxim's own special pâté—Terrine Maxim's. Hot hors d'oeuvres include a fragrant Soufflé au fromage and Feuillete de Fruits de Mer (puff pastry filled with seafood with lobster sauce).

A specialty entrée of the Paris Maxim's that is also served here is the Sole Albert. Also fresh from the sea is la Fleur de Turbot au Cerfeuil, sauce choron et sauce champagne (turbot baked with chervil in a pastry crust, with two sauces). If you prefer meat or poultry try the Poulet Sauté au Marjolaine (chicken cooked with fresh marjoram), or Pigeonneau au Porto sur ris de veau (squab in Port wine, served on a bed of sweetbreads).

Another direct import from the original Maxim's is a dessert entitled crepe veuve joyeuse. This is a French pancake for two, stuffed with lemon soufflé. Soufflé Givre Maxim's is this restaurant's special cold soufflé.

Luncheon at Maxim's is served Monday through Saturday. Dinner is served every night. Reservations are urged. Gentlemen are requested to wear jackets and ties. All major credit cards are honored. Prices range from medium to expensive.

SOLE ALBERT

4 whole soles, 12 ounces (336 grams) each

5 ounces (150 milliliters) clarified butter

1/2 pound (224 grams) fresh white bread crumbs

1/2 cup (120 milliliters) water

1 ounce (28 grams) chopped shallots

1 cup (240 milliliters) vermouth

1/2 cup (120 milliliters) white wine

1 tablespoon (15 milliliters) beef glaze

1 pound (454 grams) softened butter

salt and pepper, to taste

2 teaspoons (10 milliliters) diced lobster

Place the soles in a pan with the clarified butter. Place bread crumbs on top and brown under the broiler. Add the water and bake in the oven at 350° for 10 minutes. Remove the soles from the pan and keep warm.

Add the shallots, vermouth, white wine, and beef glaze to the butter in the pan and reduce to almost dry. Beat, then add the remaining butter, salt and pepper to taste. Strain well, then add the diced lobster and sauté it briefly in the butter.

To serve, place the sauce in a platter and set the soles on top.

Serves: 4

Le Bon Vivant,

222 Greenwood Avenue
Glenview, Illinois 60025
(312) 967-1222

Proprietor: Jovan Pajich

Le Bon Vivant, Ltd. presents fine traditional French/Continental cuisine in an elegant setting. There are three gracious dining rooms. The Garden Room—a good bet for lunch—features an array of hanging plants and white wrought-iron furniture. On either side of this room are located formal dining rooms decorated in black and white, with beamed ceilings, chandeliers, and antique china servers as decorations.

Cold appetizers include jumbo shrimps, thin sliced smoked salmon from Scotland, genuine Beluga Malossol Caviar, or a thick slice of smooth, country-style pâté maison. Hot delicacies include Crepes Royales—crepes stuffed with shrimps, lobster, crab, glazed with lobster sauce—and such standards as Oysters Rockefeller and Coquilles St. Jacques. A savory baked French onion soup completes the list.

The fragrance of garlic arises from the entrée Fruits from the Sea Monte Carlo—an interesting combination of lobster, shrimp, crabmeat sautéed in lemon butter with green pepper, olive, artichoke, garlic, and white wine. There is a whole English Dover Sole Belle Meunière, served with lemon, butter and mushrooms; Lobster Thermidor; and the Scampi Provençale—large shrimps sautéed in lemon butter with mushrooms, garlic, tomatoes, and herbs.

A specialty at Le Bon Vivant is Steak Diane, prepared at your table, and there is Veal Oscar garnished with crabmeat, asparagus and sauce Béarnaise, as well as a fine Duck à l'Orange (roast duckling flambé with Grand Marnier and served with orange sauce). A few of the flaming dessert offerings are Crepes Suzette, Cherries Jubilee, and Bananas Foster.

Le Bon Vivant is open for lunch and dinner Tuesday through Sunday. Reservations are a must. Gentlemen are required to wear jackets. All major credit cards are welcomed. Prices are expensive.

Ltd.

STEAK DIANE

14 ounces (392 grams) beef tenderloin

2 teaspoons (10 milliliters) clarified butter

salt and pepper, to taste

5 butter chips

1 teaspoon (5 milliliters) shallots, chopped

1/4 teaspoon (1.25 milliliters) Dijon mustard

1/2 cup (120 milliliters) fresh mushrooms, sliced

1/4 teaspoon (1.25 milliliters) fresh garlic, chopped

cognac, for flaming

3/4 cup (180 milliliters) demi-glaze or basic brown sauce

1 ounce (30 milliliters) red wine, Bordeaux or Burgundy

1 teaspoon (5 milliliters) Escoffier sauce

1/4 teaspoon (1.25 milliliters) Worcestershire sauce

1 teaspoon (5 milliliters) fresh parsley, chopped

Brush the meat with clarified butter, then brown in a heated pan and season with salt and pepper. Remove meat from the pan and add 2 chips of butter and the shallots. Sauté for 2 minutes. Add the mustard and mushrooms and sauté for 30 seconds. Add the garlic and sauté for an additional 30 seconds.

Place the meat back in the pan and flame with cognac. Add the demi-glaze sauce, red wine, Escoffier sauce, and Worcestershire sauce. Sauté until meat reaches the desired degree of doneness. Add the remaining butter and chopped parsley. When the butter melts, the meat is ready to serve. Suggestion: serve Steak Diane with wild rice and a garnish of watercress.

Serves: 2

Wine: *Romanée, St. Vivant, 1969*

For over 17 years, the **Farmer's Daughter** has offered unusual Continental dining in a relaxed, elegant atmosphere. The original Spanish decor is now being replaced with Victorian touches: lace curtains, massive antique pieces, copper accents. Remodeling added a cocktail lounge and two dance floors. And dining is available in their courtyard if you make reservations.

Owner Kandy Norton Henely keeps a close eye on what patrons order and frequently adjusts her menu in accordance with those dictates. For example, when she noticed that soups and salads were gaining in popularity, she added some lunch items to the dinner menu. This made less expensive, lighter meals available throughout the day.

The Farmer's Daughter has always been regarded for miles around as the place to go for those unusual menu items, the small extra touches that can make a classic entrée seem new. Those entrées might be Wiener Schnitzel, Chicken Kiev, French Tournedos Dijon, Creole short ribs, or Dover sole. Those extra touches: cheddar cheese beer soup, warm date bread, banana muffins, a salad with fruit and nuts, fried potato skins, and other surprising concoctions.

Ms. Henely also encourages patrons to tour her kitchen. "Book reservations with me, but be prepared to work the day through from dishes to desserts. Apron furnished," she says in earnest.

The Farmer's Daughter is open seven days for lunch and dinner. Call ahead for reservations and dress neatly. Major credit cards are accepted and prices are bargains.

Farmer's Daughter

14455 La Grange Road
Orland Park, Illinois 60462
(312) 349-7799

Proprietor/Chef: Kandy Norton Henely

IRISH WHISKEY PIE

1 1/2 teaspoons (7.5 milliliters) unflavored gelatin

1/2 cup (120 milliliters) cold water

2 squares unsweetened chocolate

1/2 cup (120 milliliters) hot water

1/4 teaspoon (1.25 milliliters) salt

1/2 cup (120 milliliters) sugar

1/4 cup (60 milliliters) egg yolks

1/4 cup (60 milliliters) milk

3 tablespoons (45 milliliters) Irish whiskey

1/4 cup (60 milliliters) egg whites

1 cup (240 milliliters) heavy cream, whipped

1/4 cup (60 milliliters) sliced almonds

1 baked 9-inch (23-centimeter) pastry shell, chilled

whipped cream and sliced almonds, to garnish

Dissolve the gelatin in cold water. Combine the chocolate, hot water, salt, and sugar. Bring to a boil and cook until smooth. Mix the egg yolks and milk, then stir into the chocolate mixture. Melt the gelatin over hot water in a double boiler until clear, then add to the chocolate mixture along with the whiskey. Pour into a mixing bowl and place over crushed ice until syrupy. Beat the egg whites and fold in, then fold in the whipped cream and almonds. Pour into the pastry shell and chill for 4 hours. Garnish with additional whipped cream and sliced almonds before serving.

Serves: 6-8

The Glass Chimney is unusual not only because of its name, but also because owners Dieter and Hermine Puska really do live up to their pledge to serve you "one of the memorable meals of your life." The cooking, closely supervised by Dieter Puska as chef, is typical of the best of a number of major European countries, with the inspiration of France predominating.

You dine well in an atmosphere of warmth and European-style elegance. The elegance extends to the wine collection, drawn from many domestic and overseas sources, with prices ranging from $6 to $800.

Fresh fish and various seafood delicacies are prepared with care. The Saumon Farci en Chemise, Sauce Aurora (baby coho salmon, stuffed with king crabmeat and baked in puff pastry) or Filet of Sole à l'Orly (boneless fillets of lemon sole dipped in beer batter, cooked in butter, and glazed with tomato sauce and Hollandaise) are for the dedicated fish lover.

Among poultry dishes are such choices as Chicken Breast "Celeste" (chicken breast sautéed in herb butter with garlic, topped with sliced mushrooms, Hollandaise, and cheese, browned under a salamander, and served with sauce Marsala) and an exotic dish, Faisan Auf Jaegermeister-Art.

There are a goodly number of beef and veal dishes, steaks and chops, with many sporting a generous dash of wine or brandy, and several fine desserts.

The Glass Chimney serves dinner Monday through Saturday. Reservations are recommended. Jackets for men are required, but ties are not. Most major credit cards are honored. Prices range from medium to expensive.

Glass Chimney

12901 North Meridian Street
Carmel, Indiana 46032
(317) 844-0921

Proprietor/Chef: Dieter Puska

FAISAN AUF JAEGERMEISTER-ART
(Pheasant Hunters-Style)

2 3-pound (1.35-kilogram) pheasants

salt and pepper, to taste

pinch of thyme

flour, to dust

4 ounces (120 milliliters) clarified butter

12 fresh mushrooms, quartered

1/4 pound (113 grams) smoked bacon or Black Forest ham, cubed

1/2 pound (227 grams) small fresh shallots

4 juniper berries, crushed

4 bay leaves

8 ounces (240 milliliters) dry red wine, Burgundy preferred

4 cups (960 milliliters) Espagnole Sauce (brown sauce)

watercress, to garnish

Cut the pheasants in half and remove the breastbone, hip bone, and wishbone. Season with salt, pepper, and thyme and dust with flour. Add clarified butter to a preheated roasting pan or large skillet and brown the pheasants quickly to a golden brown on the skin side. Turn the pheasants over, cover with a lid, and bake in a 350° oven for approximately 10 minutes.

Remove the pheasants from the oven, drain the excess fat, and then add the mushrooms, bacon, and shallots. Add the juniper berries and bay leaves and return to the oven for another 10 minutes.

Remove the roasting pan from the oven and add red wine and Espagnole Sauce. Cover and simmer for approximately 10-15 minutes or until the birds are tender. Remove the pheasants from the pan, arrange them on a serving platter, and keep warm.

Place the pan on the top of the stove and reduce the sauce to about half the original quantity. Remove the bay leaves and spoon the sauce over the pheasants. Serve piping hot, garnished with watercress. Suggestion: serve with parsley potatoes.

Serves: 4

Wine: *Light white Rhine or Moselle, California Chardonnay or white Burgundy*

Cafe

What was once "Big John's Carryout"—a barbecue chicken and ribs and later pizza parlor—is now one of America's premier French restaurants: **Cafe Johnell**, named for its founder and owner John L. Spillson.

Cafe Johnell has regular customers who travel over 200 miles to have dinner in a luxurious Edwardian atmosphere that features burgundy, pink, and peach colors, soft lights and music, an original art collection with some paintings dating back to the 17th century, and a fabulous wine cellar—one of the most complete in the country with international wines ranging in price from $6 to $1500 and vintages up to 170 years old. John travels the world and personally selects the wines. He also helps select the ingredients for the superb dishes prepared by his

daughter Nike, who is a graduate of Le Cordon Bleu in Paris.

Dinner at Cafe Johnell is an evening out and usually takes four or more hours. The restaurant serves only 90 patrons, and there is normally only one turnover per night. The cuisine is classic French using only the finest ingredients: fish from Scotland, Boston, New York, and Florida; corn-fed beef aged 21 days; Wisconsin Dutch Valley milk-fed veal; fresh vegetables and seasonings.

The restaurant is open Monday through Friday for lunch and dinner and on Saturday for dinner. Reservations are a must. Jackets are required for men and all major credit cards are accepted. Prices are moderate to moderately expensive.

Johnell

2529 South Calhoun Street
Fort Wayne, Indiana 46807
(219) 456-1939

Proprietor: John Spillson
Chef: Nike Spillson

CANETONS AUX POIRES BELLE NIKE
(Roasted Ducklings with Red Wine Sauce and Fresh Poached Pears)

3 cups (90 milliliters) red wine

1 cup (30 milliliters) orange juice

1 1/2 cups (360 milliliters) sugar

1 cinnamon stick

6 whole cloves

6 large, firm pears, peeled, stems left on

1 lemon, cut in half

6 cups (1.4 liters) brown stock

3 4 1/2-pound (2-kilogram) Long Island-style ducklings

salt and white pepper, to taste

boiling water, as needed

2 tablespoons (30 milliliters) arrowroot

2 tablespoons (30 milliliters) cold water

1 small bunch of parsley

To poach the pears: in a pot that will just hold the pears comfortably, bring the red wine, orange juice, sugar, cinnamon stick, and cloves to a boil. Reduce the heat and allow them to simmer. Trim the bottoms of the pears flat so they will stand upright without falling over. Rub the peeled pears with the lemon half to prevent discoloration. Add the pears to the simmering red wine syrup and poach for 10 minutes. Remove the pot from the heat and allow to cool.

In a separate pot, reduce the brown stock to 2 cups (480 milliliters).

To roast the ducklings: remove and discard any fat from the interior of the ducks. Clip the wings at the first joint. Trim off some of the skin from the neck. Season the inside and outside of the ducks with salt and pepper. Blanche the ducks in a large pot of boiling water for 5 minutes. Remove them from the boiling water and drain. Season a second time with salt and pepper. Place ducks in a roasting pan with a raised rack and bake in a preheated 325° oven for 2 1/2 hours or until done. Ducks will be tender and their skin very crisp.

To prepare the sauce: combine 2 cups (480 milliliters) of the red wine pear syrup and the reduced brown stock and bring to a boil. Dissolve the arrowroot in cold water and add to the boiling sauce to thicken it. Sauce should coat the back of a spoon and be very shiny. Strain the sauce through a chinois and keep hot in a water bath.

Reheat the pears in the remaining syrup on top of the stove in a covered pot.

To serve: coat 1 cup (240 milliliters) of sauce on a serving platter large enough to hold the ducks. Garnish with poached pears and parsley. Serve the remaining sauce on the side. Carve the ducks at tableside, nap each half with sauce, and serve each portion with a poached pear.

Serves: 6

Wine: *Beaujolais or a light Burgundy*

Joe Muer's Restaurant

Proprietors: Joe, Tom,
Bill, and Grandmother Muer

2000 Gratiot Avenue
Detroit, Michigan 48207
(313) 567-1088

Joe Muer's Restaurant means seafood to natives of Detroit, just as that city represents the automobile industry to the rest of the nation. Joe Muer, Sr., opened a little oyster bar 50 years ago, and today, three generations later, the Muer family has developed that restaurant into an institution that maintains the highest quality standards while serving an average of 1,200 meals a day and 10,000 pounds of seafood a week.

This huge restaurant seems smaller than it really is because it's divided into rooms of various sizes and shapes. All share a decor of brick, oak, beamed ceilings, and stained glass.

Andrew Toth is only the third chef in the restaurant's entire 50-year history. His special touch is evident right at the start of your meal in appetizers such as Scallops à la Muer, Oysters à la Ernie, Fruits of the Sea for two, and Shrimp Ilene with a sauce of butter, garlic, almonds, sherry, and parsley.

Joe Muer's specializes in the presentation of large portions of good fish that are simply prepared and served fresh, moist, and tender. Most of the two dozen seafood entrées listed daily are broiled, fried, poached, or steamed in an uncomplicated manner. Offerings usually include Great Lakes whitefish, pickerel, trout, smelts, perch, halibut, Dover sole, bluefish, haddock, and Pacific salmon. During the winter months, the many shellfish dishes are augmented by stone crabs flown in from Florida.

Joe Muer's Restaurant is open for lunch Monday through Friday and for dinner every day but Sunday. Reservations are not taken. Jackets are recommended. Mastercard, American Express, and Visa are honored. Prices are in the medium range.

MUER'S BEAN RELISH

2 quarts (1.9 liters) Great Northern beans

water, as needed

salt and pepper, to taste

1/2 cup (120 milliliters) minced parsley

1/2 cup (120 milliliters) minced onions

vinegar, to taste

Start the beans in cold water and cook very slowly at low heat, adding water as it boils down. (Do not pre-soak.) Occasionally, turn the beans with a wooden spoon to allow even cooking. Cooking time is hard to judge, so test occasionally by pinching a bean. When *just* soft, they are done. Remove from heat and when cool add salt, pepper, parsley, and onions. Then, mix in small amounts of vinegar, tasting as you go. Serve as an appetizer.

For future use, the cooked beans can be stored in their own juice in the refrigerator without the seasonings and vinegar.

Serves: 8-10

The **London Chop House** has a warm, inviting personality that draws people from all over Detroit and nearby Canada to savor its American and Continental cuisine. The vast menu, which changes daily, features many old favorites and reflects the chef's French training.

Important contributions to the general English decor are the oil paintings, soft napery in paisley patterns, and a great long bar that takes up almost one whole side of the dining room.

You can sample Chef Schmidt's *nouvelle cuisine* in one of the hot appetizers—Oysters in Champagne Sauce. A surprisingly tasty House-Smoked Lake Superior Trout is recommended as an unusual cold appetizer.

Seafood entrées include Gaujonettes of Dover Sole Murat sautéed with fresh mushrooms, tomato, potato and artichoke; and the House-Made Green Fettucini with Maine Sea Scallops and Oysters.

The obvious specialties of the house are the beef entrées. The USDA Prime Beef, dry-aged and char-broiled, is the finest in the area as are the filet mignon, sirloin steak, and Chateaubriand Bouquetière. They also serve Thin Schnitzel Beef Sirloin and Jim Beard's Hamburger Steak garlic scented, with cracked black peppercorns, and flamed with brandy.

Many imported and domestic wines are listed on the reverse side of the lunch and dinner menus. New wines are offered each month.

The London Chop House is open for lunch and dinner, Monday through Saturday. Reservations are recommended. Jackets and ties for men are required. All major credit cards are honored. Prices run from modest to moderately expensive.

London Chop House

155 West Congress
Detroit, Michigan 48226
(313) 962-0277

Chef: Jimmy Schmidt

MAIN SEA SCALLOPS AND GREAT SALT BAY OYSTERS IN BASIL BUTTER SAUCE

2 ounces (60 milliliters) shallots, chopped coarsely

pinch of thyme leaves

1 bay leaf

1 bunch parsley stems

1 bunch fresh basil, preferably fine leaf, with stems

2 ounces (60 milliliters) white peppercorns, cracked

1 bottle white wine, Pinot Chardonnay preferred

1/2 quart (470 milliliters) heavy cream

salt, white pepper, and cayenne pepper, to taste

1 pound (454 grams) Maine Sea Scallops, cleaned and sliced 1/4 inch (.6 centimeter) thick

24 Salt Bay Oysters, shucked, liquid strained and reserved

2-4 ounces (60-120 milliliters) unsalted butter

3-4 sweet red peppers, fine julienne

1 bunch watercress, to garnish (optional)

To prepare the acid reduction: combine the shallots, thyme, bay leaf, parsley stems, basil stems, white peppercorns, and 3/4 bottle of wine in an acid-resistant pan. Reduce over medium heat to 1/4 of the original volume. When reduced, strain immediately through a fine strainer and reserve.

In a separate pan, reduce the heavy cream to half its original volume or until thick. Reserve.

Bring the acid reduction to a rapid boil. Slowly blend in the reduced cream while quickly whisking. Reduce to sauce consistency. Season with the salt and peppers to taste. When mixture reaches sauce consistency, add the scallops to poach lightly. When the scallops turn opaque, add the oysters and their liquid. Allow the edges of the oysters to curl slightly. Immediately, remove the scallops and the oysters with a slotted spoon to a strainer to drain.

Reduce the sauce back to the proper silky texture while adding the butter, tablespoon by tablespoon. Check the seasonings. (If, during this reduction, the sauce starts to get heavy or the butter separates, add small amounts of the remaining white wine.) When sauce consistency is reached, add the red peppers and the fresh basil. Combine well and add the scallops and oysters. Combine, then pull immediately off heat and pour into a stainless steel bowl and whisk slightly to stabilize the butter temperature. Serve immediately.

Serves: 4

Wine: *Pinot Chardonnay, Mayacamas, 1977*

Win Schuler's

Chef: Marge Hakes

115 South Eagle Street
Marshall, Michigan 49068
(616) 781-3961

Win Schuler's, a 72-year-old official Michigan historic site, is a handsome family-style restaurant serving American favorite dishes. Under Schuler family ownership and management from the start, the restaurant present an early American appearance with its entrance portico, white widow's walk above, and carriage lights on either side.

The main dining room sports ceiling beams inscribed with quotations related to the enjoyment of food and drink, and wall murals depict historic Marshall buildings and events. In the Inner Circle, a smaller dining room, the smart yet warm feeling is enhanced by the semi-circular, two-tier table seating arrangement with red velvet banquettes overlooking a pit area with a tiled fireplace. Tablecloths are burgundy with wide white stripes. Smoked mirror walls reflect hanging lamps with pleated silk shades and deep red and burgundy furnishings. The Courtyard Room presents a light, airy aspect with skylights, a glass wall facing onto a patio, other walls of white brick, plants, and a generally light decor. The bar is like an old English tavern and serves drinks and light meals.

The Corn & Crabmeat Chowder is a good way to start your dinner. Another, Schuler's Thick Swiss Onion Soup, is a hearty treat, laced with a touch of beer and topped with Mozzarella cheese. The Schuler Salad consists of shrimp, Swiss cheese, crisp bacon bits, croutons, and a house dressing served over fresh tossed garden greens.

Among the beef entrées, a favorite is Roast Prime Rib of Beef, aged and cut in Schuler's own butcher shop, served as you like it. (A limited number of end cuts are available each evening.) Alaskan King Crab Legs are served with drawn butter, and there's always a daily fresh fish special.

Lunch is served at Win Schuler's Monday through Saturday. Dinner is served every day, and there is a Sunday brunch. Reservations are advised. Jackets and ties for men are recommended. Most major credit cards are honored. Prices range from bargains to moderate.

WINE PIE

1/2 pound (227 grams) raisins

1/4 cup (60 milliliters) water

1/4 cup (60 milliliters) vermouth

3/4 cup (180 milliliters) sweet vermouth

1/2 pound (227 grams) vanilla instant pudding mix

1 1/4 cup (300 milliliters) milk

1/2 pint (240 milliliters) whipping cream

1 1/4 ounces (35 grams) chopped nuts

1 9-inch (23-centimeter) graham cracker pie crust

Soak the raisins overnight in the water and 1/3 the vermouth, then drain. Prepare the vanilla pudding using the milk and the remaining vermouth. Whip the cream and fold it into the pudding with the nuts and drained raisins. Pour this mixture into the prepared pie crust and freeze until firm. To serve, thaw slightly and decorate with whipped cream.

Serves: 6-8

Wine: *Asti Spumante*

Camelot is a recreation of a 15th-century English castle. The restaurant's interior is as authentic-looking as its exterior: dark, heavy chestnut and oak furniture and paneling, red and black upholstery, and window coverings, medieval armor and weaponry, English pewter and silver, stone walls, candlelight merge to considerable effect. Unlike establishments where clever decorating overshadows the cuisine, dining at Camelot stands out as a complete experience.

To say that the food is authentic would be an injustice. Frankly, the knights and ladies of old Camelot never had it this good. The recreated Camelot will satisfy any gourmet's fantasy. Although the prime rib is the best seller, this restaurant is also known for its fish specialties such as delicately prepared Whole Dover Sole, Sauté Meunière, or fresh Wall-eyed Pike, Véronique. Other well prepared dishes are Côte de Veau, Normande, served with Minnesota wild rice; Le Caneton Entier aux Pêches Flambé, carved at tableside; and outstanding Le Coeur de Filet Sauté Diane; among others. Prix fixe dinners are also available and include, for a very reasonable sum, everything from hors d'oeuvres to a selection of desserts including excellent Chocolate Mousse and English Trifle. A choice of wine from Camelot's comprehensive cellar is additional.

Camelot is open for lunch and dinner, Monday through Saturday. Reservations are suggested. Jackets and ties are preferred. Major credit cards are accepted. Prices are moderately expensive.

Camelot

5300 West 78th Street
Bloomington, Minnesota
(612) 835-2455

Proprietor: Hans J. Skalle

CREPES SUZETTE

2/3 cup (16 milliliters) flour

1 tablespoon (15 milliliters) sugar

pinch of salt

2 whole eggs

2 egg yolks

1 3/4 cups (420 milliliters) milk

2 tablespoons (30 milliliters) melted butter

1 tablespoon (15 milliliters) rum or cognac

butter, as needed

1/2 cup (120 milliliters) sugar

8 ounces (240 milliliters) fresh orange juice

peel of orange (include some of the yellow)

peel of lemon (include some of the yellow)

1/8 pound (56 grams) sweet butter

1 ounce (30 milliliters) Benedictine

1 ounce (30 milliliters) yellow Chartreuse

1 ounce (30 milliliters) cognac

To prepare the batter for crepes: sift together the flour, 1 tablespoon (15 milliliters) sugar, and salt. Beat together the eggs and egg yolks and add them to the dry ingredients. Add milk and stir the mixture until it is smooth. Add 2 tablespoons (30 milliliters) melted butter and rum or cognac. Let the batter stand for 2 hours before using.

To cook the crepes: melt just enough butter in a hot pan to coat it thinly. Pour in a thin layer of crepe batter. The crepe should set and become brown in about 1 minute. Turn it over to brown the other side. Yields: approximately 12 crepes.

To prepare the sauce: caramelize the 1/2 cup (120 milliliters) sugar lightly, making sure it does not burn. Add the orange juice, peels, and sweet butter. Reduce the sauce to about 1/3.

Add the crepes, one by one, to the sauce, turning them over so they are well saturated. Fold or roll the crepes. Pour the Benedictine, yellow Chartreuse, and cognac over them. Ignite and serve quickly, pouring the sauce over the finished crepes.

Serves: 6

Wine: *Champagne*

Charlie's Cafe Exceptionale

Proprietor: Louise H. Saunders

701 Fourth Avenue South
Minneapolis, Minnesota 55415
(612) 335-8851

Charlie's Cafe Exceptionale is located in its own handsome English Tudor-style building and is really a complex of separate dining rooms. The main floor contains The Fireside Cocktail Lounge set around a massive fireplace. There are five oak paneled rooms. The Hunt Room, Oak Room, and the Studio are formal in atmosphere. The Dub Room, with its own small bar, is informal. The Pub Room features a 22-foot oil mural of old English themes. Upstairs there are several private banquet rooms.

Charlie's Cafe takes good care of you—an accomplishment when you realize that they serve several hundred thousand meals each year.

A favorite among other choice appetizers is the Deluxe Hors D'Oeuvres Tray for two. It is a truly impressive array of shrimp with cocktail sauce, liver pâté with remoulade sauce, marinated herring, smoked oysters, corned beef, and other delicacies.

The Roast Peppered Rib Eye of Beef with piquant sauce is a well-known Charlie's specialty. The Teriyaki Tenderloin en Brochette marinated in an Oriental sauce, broiled with mushroom caps, and served with saffron rice and fresh pineapple, is just as it should be, tender and flavorful.

In the way of seafood, there's Charlie's Well of the Sea (a combination of shellfish), a tender Filet of Walleyed Pike with toasted almonds, and baked Rainbow Trout with Minnesota wild rice and crabmeat filling.

There are several rich desserts, including Strawberries Acapulco for two—crepes filled with fresh strawberries, a sauce of butter, brown sugar, Kirschwasser, Cointreau and rum, topped with vanilla ice cream and flamed at tableside.

Charlie's Cafe Exceptionale serves lunch Monday through Friday and dinner Monday through Saturday. Reservations are a must. Informal attire is called for in the Dub Room, but gentlemen are asked to wear jackets and ties in the other dining rooms. All major credit cards are honored. Prices are moderately expensive.

ROAST PEPPERED RIB EYE OF BEEF

5-6 pounds (2.25-2.7 kilograms) boneless rib eye of beef

1/2 cup (120 milliliters) black pepper, coarsely cracked

1/2 teaspoon (2.5 milliliters) ground cardamom

1 tablespoon (15 milliliters) tomato paste

1/2 teaspoon (2.5 milliliters) garlic powder

1 teaspoon (5 milliliters) paprika

1 cup (240 milliliters) soy sauce

3/4 cup (180 milliliters) vinegar

1 cup (240 milliliters) water

1 1/2 tablespoons (22.5 milliliters) cornstarch (optional)

1/4 cup (60 milliliters) water (optional)

Trim the fat from the beef. Combine the pepper and cardamom and rub all over the beef and press into the meat with the heel of the hand. Place the roast in a shallow baking pan.

To prepare the marinade: mix the tomato paste, garlic powder, and paprika together. Gradually add soy sauce, then vinegar, then pour over the meat and refrigerate overnight.

Spoon the marinade over the meat, then remove the meat from the marinade. Reserve the marinade and let the meat stand at room temperature for 1 hour.

Wrap the meat in foil and place in a shallow pan. Roast in a 300° oven for 1 1/2 hours for a medium rare roast. Open the foil and reserve the drippings. Brown the roast, uncovered, at 350° while making the gravy.

To prepare the gravy: strain the drippings and skim off the excess fat. Mix 1 cup (240 milliliters) of skimmed meat juice and 1 cup (240 milliliters) of water and bring to a boil. Correct the seasoning with a little marinade.

Serve the roast *au jus*, or thicken the gravy with the cornstarch mixed with cold water. Suggestion: serve with wild rice.

Serves: 8-10

The Blue Horse, named after Seattle artist Roland Terry's metal sculpture, is owned by Clifford Warling, who has recently celebrated his 50th year in the restaurant business. In December 1964, he and wife, Jean, opened this beautiful establishment that features Continental cuisine served in the warm atmosphere of bricks, mirrors, and wood paneling.

Food preparation is administered by executive chef Thomas Reilly, who has been with the restaurant for 12 years. The house specialties, Tartare Steak à la Blue Horse and Roast Fillet of Beef-Perigourdine highlight a superb menu which also includes Duckling à l'Orange (flamed in Grand Marnier), shellfish, salmon, and superb Fetuccine Alfredo. And special requests will be honored. Your meal may be complemented with your choice of an imported or domestic wine from a modest, but certainly adequate list.

The Blue Horse is open 11:00 a.m. — 1:00 a.m. Monday through Friday, and 4:00 p.m. — 1:00 a.m. Saturday. Jackets are required in the evening. Because the seating capacity is only 135, reservations are suggested. All major credit cards are accepted. Prices are moderate.

Blue Horse

1355 University Avenue
St. Paul, Minnesota 55104
(612) 871-8900

Proprietor: Clifford Warling
General Manager: John Warling

ROAST FILLET OF BEEF-PERIGOURDINE

2 pounds (908 grams) beef tenderloin

flour, to dust

salt, pepper, and Ac'cent, to taste

1/2 cup (120 milliliters) butter or cooking oil

1/3 cup (80 milliliters) finely minced onions, celery, and carrots (garlic optional)

1/3 cup (80 milliliters) flour

2 cans undiluted beef consommé

1 teaspoon (5 milliliters) tomato paste

1/3 cup (80 milliliters) Madeira wine

watercress, to garnish

diced goose liver pâté and truffles, to decorate

1/8 cup (30 milliliters) chopped truffles

Dust the meat in flour and season it with salt, pepper, and Ac'cent. Sear the meat in butter or oil until brown on all sides. Remove the meat from the pan and add the minced onions, celery, and carrots (and garlic, if desired) to the drippings and sear.

Brown the 1/3 cup (80 milliliters) flour in a pie tin in a 350° oven and add to the mixture in the pan. Then add the beef consommé and the tomato paste. Let simmer for 8-10 minutes, stirring occasionally.

Place the beef tenderloin in a small roaster and strain the sauce over the meat. Loosen the scrapings with Madeira wine and strain into the roaster. Roast the meat to the desired degree of doneness.

Place the roast on a platter, garnish with watercress, and decorate the whole tenderloin with pâté and truffles. Keep the sauce warm, add chopped truffles, and serve in a sauce boat.

Serves: 4

Wine: *Chateau Montelana Cabernet Sauvignon, 1976*

American Restaurant, located in the heart of the nation, draws its culinary inspiration from all corners of the United States. Its romantic setting is designed to resemble a huge lace valentine. This effect is achieved with a fan-shaped network of glass and oak bentwood canopies in a dining room graced by a profusion of clear filament lamps and sprays of lights at the windows. Shimmering reflections, a dramatic view of the city, and soft music in the background add to the air of romance. The ambiance is completed with theatrical projector lamps throwing showers of dappled light across the room.

Your choice of wine at dinner will be drawn from an extensive list of imported and domestic entries, with the emphasis on California vineyards. The prix fixe dinner includes a choice of soup and an entrée (Peppered Duck with Figs in Red Port with Almond Rice, or Jambalaya of Oysters with Smoked Sausage and Spiced Chicken, for example). A Spinach Salad with Hot Bacon Dressing and a selection from the dessert buffet and a beverage are also included.

The fish of the day may be ordered grilled, poached, or sautéed, with Grits Timbale. You will also find Trout from the Ozarks with Barbeque Chive Butter and Zucchini Custard, and Atlantic Salmon, poached and served with clams, shrimp, mussels, and saffron dressing.

Prime Kansas City Steak may be ordered double thick. The Tenderloin Steak comes smothered with onions or red wine sauce.

Luncheon is served weekdays, dinner is served Monday through Saturday. Reservations are advised. Gentlemen are requested to wear jackets. Credit cards honored are American Express, Mastercard, and Visa. Prices range from moderate to moderately expensive.

American Restaurant

Crown Center
25th and Grand Avenue
Kansas City, Missouri 64108
(816) 471-8050

Proprietor:
American Food Service Enterprises, Inc.
Chef: Bradley Ogden

SUGARBUSH MOUNTAIN MAPLE MOUSSE

1/4 cup (60 milliliters) cold water

2 1/4 teaspoons (11.25 milliliters) Knox unflavored gelatin

1/2 cup (120 milliliters) Log Cabin maple syrup

2 fresh egg yolks

1/4 cup (60 milliliters) light brown sugar

1/2 tablespoon (7.5 milliliters) Mapeline maple flavoring

2 fresh egg whites

1 cup (240 milliliters) cold heavy cream

1/2 teaspoon (2.5 milliliters) pure vanilla extract

Combine the water and gelatin in a large stainless steel mixing bowl. Add the maple syrup and stir to blend.

In the bowl of an electric mixer, whip the egg yolks until thick and lemon-colored. Add the brown sugar and continue whipping until all is evenly blended. Pour the mixture into a heavy-bottomed saucepan along with the gelatin/syrup mixture. Cook over moderate heat until thickened and coats the back of a spoon. Remove from heat and allow to cool.

Add the flavoring and mix into the cooked egg yolk mixture.

Place the egg whites in the bowl of an electric mixer and whip on high speed until stiff peaks are formed.

In a separate mixing bowl, whip the cream with the vanilla to form stiff peaks. Fold the cream and egg whites into the cooled egg yolk mixture, being careful not to over mix. Divide the finished mousse into 6 egg-shaped molds. Cover the molds with plastic wrap and refrigerate until well-chilled and completely set. Unmold just prior to serving.

Serves: 6

Jasper's Restaurant's northern Italian, French, and Continental cuisine is presented in a baroque atmosphere of old-world elegance with a plush decor featuring fine German woodwork, English carpeting, Venetian draps, Louis XV furniture, delicate Murano crystal, and tables graced by gold-colored linen, fresh flowers, and candles.

The wine cellar contains 85 internationally known wines and regional favorites.

Cold appetizers—the Antipasti Freddi—offer Prosciutto Di Parma et Melon and Antipasto Italiano for two or more. Among the hot Hors D'Oeuvres are the house specialties Escargots à la Bourguignonne and Gambere a La Livornese. There are also several fine pasta appetizers.

Owner/chef Jasper Mirabile recommends Vitello Limonata con Melazana Dore.

Scallopine Don Salvatore is a favorite of mine: scallop of veal cooked with a bit of garlic, artichoke hearts and Bordelaise sauce over wild rice.

The Entrecôte au Poivre Flambé (Kansas City sirloin flamed tableside in a crushed peppercorn sauce) and Filet de Boeuf Oscar (broiled tenderloin with crabmeat and white asparagus, topped with Bordelaise sauce) are house specialties. Lobster Livornese con Risotto (lobster sautéed with garlic, heavy cream and spices over wild rice) is a mild, delicious seafood entrée.

Luncheon is served Monday through Friday, and dinner Monday through Saturday. Reservations are recommended. Jackets for men are required. Mastercard, Visa, and Diners Club cards are honored. Prices are moderately expensive.

Jasper's Restaurant

405 West 75th Street
Kansas City, Missouri
(816) 363-3003

Proprietors/Chefs:
Jasper and Leonard Mirabile

VITELLO LIMONATA CON MELANZANA DORE

8 slices veal scaloppine, about 1 1/2 pounds (680 grams)

salt and freshly ground pepper, to taste

1/2 pound (227 grams) eggplant, peeled and cut into 8 1/4-inch (.64-centimeter) rounds

flour for dredging

2 eggs, lightly beaten

1 cup (240 milliliters) fine fresh bread crumbs

1/2 cup plus 3 tablespoons (165 milliliters) peanut or corn oil

1 tablespoon (15 milliliters) butter

8 thin slices of lemon

1 teaspoon (5 milliliters) oregano

1 tablespoon (15 milliliters) finely chopped parsley

Pound the veal lightly with a flat mallet, then sprinkle with salt and pepper.

Sprinkle the sliced eggplant with salt and pepper. Dredge in flour and shake off the excess. Dip in egg, then in bread crumbs. Pat to help the crumbs adhere. Heat the 1/2 cup (120 milliliters) oil and cook the eggplant pieces on both sides until golden. Drain on paper towels.

Dip the veal in the flour and shake off the excess. Dip in egg and coat each piece completely. Heat the 3 tablespoons (45 milliliters) of oil and the butter in a skillet and cook the veal, 2 at a time, until golden on each side.

Arrange the veal on a platter, slightly overlapping the slices. Top each slice with an eggplant round and a lemon slice. Sprinkle with oregano and parsley and serve hot.

Serves: 4

Wine: *Candida Frascati*

Port St. Louis

15 North Central Avenue
Clayton, Missouri 63105
(314) 727-1142

Port St. Louis prepares seafood to satisfy the most discriminating gourmet. Their artistry in cooking is equalled by the elegance and authentic detail of the opulent Victorian decor. There are fine old fireplaces, rare stained glass, and antiques in the North Room and South Room dining areas; a divider of wood and metal filagree in the bar made from antique doors from a Parisian bistro; and other tasteful accents throughout.

Port St. Louis offers a wide variety of seafood appetizers. They serve oysters five different ways, and they've got a platter of assorted cold shellfish for two. The soups are delicious, especially the Port St. Louis Creole Gumbo.

The most popular entrée is the Fresh Lemon Sole Birds, stuffed with shrimp and crab and sprinkled with cheese. Really good, too, is Thermidor of Maine Lobster. The Stuffed Flounder is filled with fresh crabmeat, chopped vegetables, and spices. Their Filet of Pompano simmers beneath a sauce of lobster, mushrooms, and red wine.

You'll also find Steak au Poivre, Tenderloin en Brochette, Porterhouse, Steak Royal, Port St. Louis Strip, Filet Mignon, Steak Diane Flambé, and Chateaubriand Bouquetière for two.

"Our Own Cheesecake" with berries, Mimi's Mousse au Chocolate, Bananas Foster Flambé, and Cherries Jubilee are favorite desserts.

Port St. Louis is open for dinner every day, closing only on major holidays. Reservations are advised. Gentlemen must wear jackets. All major credit cards are honored. Prices are moderately expensive.

CHOCOLATE MOUSSE

**1 6-ounce (168-gram) package
chocolate chips, Nestles preferred**

6 egg yolks

6 tablespoons (90 milliliters) sugar

6 tablespoons (90 milliliters) milk

1 teaspoon (5 milliliters) vanilla

6 egg whites

**1 pint (470 milliliters) whipping
cream**

Melt the chocolate over a double boiler. In a separate bowl, beat the egg yolks, sugar, and milk together, then add to the melted chocolate. Stir over low heat until very thick and smooth. Remove from heat and cool. Add the vanilla to the cooled mixture.

Whip the egg whites until they form stiff peaks, then gently fold into the cooled chocolate mixture. Whip the whipping cream and fold into the mixture. Refrigerate about 4-5 hours before serving.

Serves: 8

Maisonette has been one of the most esteemed French restaurants in the United States for more than 25 years. You are welcomed into a relaxing elegant atmosphere enhanced by glowing candles, crystal chandeliers, oil paintings, and fine china. The personal attention and service is on the same level as the superb haute cuisine.

Chef Haidon's considerable creativity is evident in one of my favorite cold hors d'oeuvres, Les Trois Pâtés Maison (three slices of pâté: one veal; another a dark, coarsely chopped blend of duck, chicken, quail, and pheasant; the third a light-colored, finely chopped pâté of pike, salmon, and scallops).

The entrées are almost an embarrassment of riches. There are Les Filets de Sole au Caviar de Saumon, Les Coquilles St. Jacques Ambassadeur ou Sautées au Naturel (fresh scallops poached on a bed of puréed mushrooms with white wine sauce), and Fillet of Brill in Crust.

Consistent beef favorites include Le Filet de Boeuf Wellington with Sauce Periguex for two, and Les Tournedos au Poivre Rose de Madagascar.

For a light meal, La Poitrine de Faisan Grand Veneur (breast of baby pheasant in a red wine sauce and garnished with apple and cranberry) or Les Aiguillettes de Caneton aux Oranges et Kiwis are outstanding preparations.

The pastry cart carries an array of flaky napoleons, cakes, tortes, and other delicate French pastries, and there are many fine dessert crepe dishes for two.

Luncheon is served at Maisonette Monday through Friday. Dinner is served Monday through Saturday. Reservations are advised. Gentlemen should wear jackets and ties. Major credit cards are honored. Prices are expensive.

Maisonette

114 East Sixth Street
Cincinnati, Ohio 45202
(513) 721-2260

Proprietors: Lee and Michael Comisar
Chef: George Haidon

FILLET OF BRILL IN CRUST

2 pounds (908 grams) brill fillets or deep sea white fish or red snapper

salt and pepper, to taste

1/2 pound (227 grams) pike fillet

6 ounces (168 grams) raw lobster meat

6 ounces (168 grams) bay shrimp

2 ounces (56 grams) truffles

2 pints (.95 liter) heavy cream

2 pounds (908 grams) puff pastry dough

2 egg yolks, thinned with water

2 cups (480 milliliters) prepared fish stock

2 tablespoons (30 milliliters) freshly chopped parsley

1 tablespoon (15 milliliters) freshly chopped chives

1/2 tablespoon (7.5 milliliters) freshly chopped tarragon

Season the fillet of brill with salt and pepper and set aside.

Purée the pike, lobster, shrimp, and truffles in a blender, then transfer to a bowl and season with salt and pepper to taste. Gradually add 1/2 the heavy cream, mix well, then spread the mixture evenly on the fillet of brill.

Spread the pastry dough 1/4 inch (.64 centimeter) thick. Lay the brill on half of it and cut the dough around it in the shape of a fish. Repeat on other half making sure that the shape is cut 2 inches (5 centimeters) larger so it can overlap the bottom part easily. Place brill between cutouts and seal overlap. Decorate the dough with the edge of a knife to imitate fish scales, fins, and the head of a fish. Brush with egg wash and bake at 375° for 20 minutes or until golden brown.

To prepare Fine Herbs Sauce: add the remaining heavy cream to the prepared fish stock and reduce to 1 1/2 cups (360 milliliters) or less. Correct the seasonings. Before serving, add the chopped parsley, chives, and tarragon.

Serve the fillet of brill in crust with sauce on the side.

Serves: 6

Wine: *California or French Chardonnay*

Au Provence Restaurant

Chef: Richard Taylor

2195 Lee Road
Cleveland Heights, Ohio
(216) 321-9511

Au Provence Restaurant is a tiny gem of a 34-seat restaurant located in a former beauty shop. In the basement, co-owner and surgeon Dr. Thomas Wykoff operates the Cedar Hill Winery, which produces 6,000 gallons of wine a year for sale. The dining room is done in a cozy, country-French style, with a high ceiling, stucco walls and archways, hand-made wooden tables, hanging plants, and soft, recorded classical music playing in the background.

The restaurant has firmly established a popularity for its French and Creole cuisine in the few years it has been open. Proprietor/Chef Richard Taylor prepares each dish with as much consideration for the eye as the palate.

Once you sit down, treat yourself to an excellent Pâté Maison, Marinated Shrimp Au Provence, Scallop and Crab Mousse, or a Continental-style serving of Port Calut Cheese with Fruits.

Two favorite entrées are the Chicken Supreme (it's served with poached fresh pears and apricot wine sauce) and the Veal Piemontaise, with artichokes and white wine sauce.

The Chocolate Mousse Au Provence is the house special dessert. Representing the old South is New Orleans Muddy Sundae, and there are also a Brandy Custard Eclair and Fresh Pineapple with Kirsch.

Dinner is served Monday through Friday with no reservations taken, and on Saturday the special gourmet dinner is by reservation only. There is no dress requirement for men. All major credit cards are accepted. Prices are moderate to moderately expensive.

VEAL CYNTHIA

2 6-ounce (168-gram) slices of white veal pounded to 1/4-inch (.64-centimeter) scallops

1/2 cup (120 milliliters) butter

salt and pepper, to taste

juice of 1 1/2 lemons

4 ounces (112 grams) Gourmandise cheese

1/4 ounce (7.5 milliliters) black truffle

chopped parsley

whole parsley, to garnish

3 slices fresh lemon, to garnish

Sauté the veal in hot butter in a sauté pan. Season with salt and pepper and squeeze the lemon juice into the pan. Reduce the pan juices to attain a balance of sweet and sour flavors. Place slices of cheese on the veal and allow to melt slightly.

When ready to serve, place the veal on a serving platter and pour the pan juices over the veal and cheese. Top with strips of truffle and chopped parsley. Garnish with whole parsley and fresh lemon slices.

Serves: 2

Wine: *Seyval Blanc*

Grenadier's Restaurant

Proprietor: Robert Jordan
Chef/General Manager: Knut Apitz

747 North Broadway
Milwaukee, Wisconsin 53202
(414) 276-0747

Grenadier's Restaurant specializes in cooking that really should be called "world-wide". Offering 17 regular entrées, several specials, and one *nouvelle cuisine* dish nightly, the menu presents authentic dishes, prepared to order and representing cuisine from around the world.

The three richly appointed dining rooms reveal an elegant, intimate appearance. Formality reigns in two of the rooms, and there is an airy, informal garden room at the back of the restaurant.

Chef/Manager Knut Apitz is willing to make suggestions gauged to your mood: a preference for light or heavy sauces, and so on.

A standout among seafood entrées is Dover Sole, prepared in the styles of Delice de Pecheur, Meunière or Almondine. A *nouvelle cuisine* specialty is Scallops and Crayfish Facon Du Chef.

Other featured entrées include Veal and Sweetbreads Basilica Ulpia with Fettucine Alfredo, Steak Diane, Lamb Curry Calcutta with Kumquats and Chutney, Wiener Schnitzel, Roast Duck Tabaka, Medallions of Veal, and Crabmeat sauté à la Grenadier, plus broiler specialties such as Chateaubriand Garni Sauce Béarnaise (for two), and Roast Rack of Lamb Garni.

Grenadier's Restaurant serves luncheon Monday through Friday, and dinner Monday through Saturday. Reservations are suggested. Gentlemen are requested to wear jackets. All major credit cards are honored. Prices are in the medium range.

GRENADIER'S ARTICHOKE SALAD

6 artichoke hearts, canned or fresh

4 ounces (112 grams) fresh pea pods

4 ounces (112 grams) fresh mushrooms

2 teaspoons (10 milliliters) Dijon mustard

1 teaspoon (5 milliliters) salt

1 teaspoon (5 milliliters) black pepper

1/4 cup (60 milliliters) red wine vinegar

1/4 cup (60 milliliters) salad oil

1 teaspoon (5 milliliters) chopped dill

1 teaspoon (5 milliliters) fresh garlic, chopped finely

1 cup (240 milliliters) half and half cream

1 ounce (56 grams) toasted sliced almonds

Cut the artichoke hearts in half and dry. Cut the fresh pea pods into 1/2-inch (1-centimeter) pieces. Slice the fresh mushrooms thinly.

To prepare the dressing: in a bowl, place the mustard, salt, pepper, red wine vinegar, salad oil, dill, and garlic. Mix well, then slowly stir in the half and half cream.

Combine the artichoke hearts, pea pods, and mushrooms and coat with the dressing. Toss carefully and then add the almonds.

Serves: 6

Karl Ratzsch's Restaurant has won many culinary awards for the superior quality of its German/Austro-Hungarian cooking under the ownership and management of the Ratzsch family since it opened 76 years ago.

There is an air of warm hospitality in this authentic replica of a Bavarian Inn. There are arched beamed ceilings, chandeliers of spreading antlers, murals, painted steins set along the walls with silver shields, wooden beer barrels, copper mugs, and a striking display of glassware. Waitresses are dressed in typically Bavarian gathered skirts, white blouses and colorful weskits.

In addition to a 22-page wine list you may choose from many of the best German beers.

House specialties of German origin include roast duckling with red cabbage and wild rice, Koenigsberger Klops (veal and pork meatballs in a Sauce Supreme of Capers, white wine,

and herbs), and from Strasbourg, roast goose shank with red cabbage and wild rice.

From a Belgian recipe comes Grenadier's Beefsteak à la Ratzsch (a thick filet mignon decked out in a sauce of mushrooms, chicken livers, and Madeira wine). Daily specialties include prime ribs of beef and broiled planked whitefish. There is also a prix fixe Special German Dinner which provides you with a sampling of a number of delicacies.

Dessert offerings include a Bavarian mocha torte, Viennese cherry strudel, chocolate schaum torte, and a nut roll à la mode with whipped rum sauce and Liederkranz.

Karl Ratzsch's serves luncheon daily except Sunday and holidays. Dinner is served every day except Christmas Eve and New Year's Day. Reservations are recommended. There are no strict dress requirements. Major credit cards are accepted. Prices are moderate to moderately expensive.

Karl Ratzsch's Restaurant

320 East Mason Street
Milwaukee, Wisconsin 53202
(414) 276-2720

Proprietor: Karl Ratzsch

BOILED BEEF BAVARIAN

3-4 pounds (1.35-1.8 kilograms) brisket of beef

6 carrots

4 stalks of celery

1 large onion

3 tablespoons (45 milliliters) salt

2 tablespoons (30 milliliters) mixed pickling spice, prepared or see instructions below

hot water, as needed

2 tablespoons (30 milliliters) butter

2 tablespoons (30 milliliters) flour

1 cup (240 milliliters) scalded milk, or 1/2 milk and 1/2 stock from boiled beef strained and skimmed

1-2 ounces (30-60 milliliters) heavy cream

3 tablespoons (45 milliliters) prepared horseradish

1 tablespoon (15 milliliters) vinegar

1 teaspoon (5 milliliters) sugar

1 teaspoon (5 milliliters) dry mustard powder

salt and white pepper, to taste

Place the first 6 ingredients in a large pot with enough hot water to cover. (If desired, pickling spice can be prepared with a mixture of mustard seed, cinnamon, ginger, bay leaf, mace, caraway, red pepper, allspice, black pepper, clove, and cardamom.) Cover the pot and simmer until the meat is tender, about 1 hour.

To prepare Horseradish Sauce: melt the butter in a saucepan at moderate heat. Add the flour and mix thoroughly. Cook for 1-2 minutes longer, then add scalded milk (or mixture of milk and stock) and stir vigorously until smooth. Continue to stir until sauce comes to a boil, but be careful to avoid scorching. Add enough cream until sauce is thick enough to coat a spoon. Add horseradish, vinegar, sugar, and dry mustard powder and bring to the boiling point, but do not boil. Adjust the seasoning with salt and white pepper.

To serve, cut the meat into 1/4-1/2-inch (.6-1.2-centimeter) slices. Arrange the slices on a warm serving plate and cover with Horseradish Sauce. Suggestion: serve with creamed spinach.

Serves: 4-6

Wine: *Gewürztraminer or a hearty beer*

Western Region

arizona

california

colorado

hawaii

oregon

the Tack Room at Rancho Del Rio

Proprietors: Fan Kane and
Mr. and Mrs. David C. Vactor
General Manager: Drew Vactor

2800 North Sabino Canyon Road
Tucson, Arizona 85715
(602) 298-2351

The Tack Room at Rancho Del Rio takes the decor of the Old West, combines it with traditional Southwestern hospitality, then serves up generous portions of award-winning Continental cuisine. The restaurant is housed in an adobe hacienda in the desert and enjoys a magnificent view of the Santa Catalina and Rincon Mountains.

They've got some very satisfying appetizers: Fresh Fruit Au Champagne, Guaymas Shrimp on Ice, Escargots Bourguignonne, Smoked Salmon, and the Tack Room's classic Spanish Gazpacho.

Tack Room Trout—fresh from Rocky Mountain rivers and filled with crabmeat dressing, Sauté Meunière—and Mexican Shrimp À La Jacques, sautéed with garlic butter, are seafood specialties that can only be found in the Southwest.

Their veal is the finest, tender Provimi-fed Wisconsin veal sauté au naturel, served with Swiss Pfifferlinge mushrooms and sherry.

Their Rack of Spring Lamb Bouquetière (surrounded with a bouquet of vegetables, flambéed, and carved at your table) is also very good.

There are all manner of steaks and chops and such haute cuisine classics as Chateaubriand Bouquetière and Beef Wellington.

A separate menu focuses on some spectacular desserts such as Chocolate Cheese Pie (a secret family recipe), chocolate or strawberry parfaits with Kahlua or Creme de Menthe, Baked Alaska, and Cherries Jubilee.

The Tack Room serves dinner only every night, with Monday closings during the summer. Reservations are suggested. Modified casual is the minimum dress standard (no blue jeans, shorts, or thongs). Visa and Mastercharge are accepted. Prices are moderate to moderately expensive.

TACK ROOM VEAL WITH PFIFFERLINGE MUSHROOMS

8 slices veal scaloppine, about 1 pound (454 grams)

salt and freshly ground pepper, to taste

2 tablespoons (30 milliliters) flour

5 tablespoons (75 milliliters) butter

1 7-ounce (196-milliliter) can of imported Pfifferlinge mushrooms, drained

1/2 cup (120 milliliters) dry sherry wine

2 tablespoons (30 milliliters) finely chopped parsley

Pound the veal slices with a flat mallet. Sprinkle with salt and pepper and dredge lightly in flour. Shake off the excess.

Heat 3 tablespoons (45 milliliters) of butter in a heavy skillet and add the veal. Cook 5-6 minutes, turning once to brown well on both sides. Remove the veal to a warm serving platter.

Add the remaining butter to the skillet and cook, stirring, until it is the color of hazelnuts. Do not burn. Add the drained mushrooms, then add the sherry and ignite it.

Pour the mushrooms and sauce over the veal, sprinkle with parsley, and serve. Suggestion: serve with baked rice.

Serves: 4

Wine: *Robert Mondavi Fumé Blanc*

Jimmy's

Proprietor: Jimmy Murphy
Chef: Otto Cloetta

201 Moreno Drive
Beverly Hills, California 90212
(213) 879-2394

Jimmy's in Beverly Hills is one of the best and most popular French restaurants in the country. It offers a strikingly attractive, romantic dining room and a similarly beautiful and comfortable outdoor patio that is open ten months out of the year. Everything at Jimmy's spells class. The linens are fine fabrics, the service is delicate china. The proprietor, Jimmy Murphy, is the classiest ingredient of all. His background includes more than three years at the Savoy Hotel in London and more than 14 years at another fine restaurant in California. Otto Cloetta, his Swiss chef, was trained in his home country, and for five years, he was head chef at one of Los Angeles's finer restaurants.

Here are a few examples of how Jimmy's takes a standard preparation and makes it all its own: The onion soup is covered with puff pastry and baked before serving, so it arrives at your table with a raised golden brown crust. The Roast Rack of Veal is served with a smooth truffle sauce, braised celery, and a cooked tomato stuffed with seasoned purée of fresh carrots. A bibb lettuce salad features a unique lemon-walnut oil cream dressing. For dessert, there's a Kiwi soufflé—made from the semi-sweet plum-like Australian fruit, with a hint of Amaretto added. The soufflé is topped with an original apricot sauce.

Jimmy's wine list is impressive; you're sure to find an imported or domestic wine appropriate for your meal. And of course, mixed drinks are served as well.

Jimmy's is open six days, for lunch and dinner on weekdays, dinner only on Saturday. Reservations are needed and jackets and ties are required evening wear. All major credit cards are honored. Prices are moderately expensive to expensive.

ONION SOUP

3 large onions

3 tablespoons (45 milliliters) butter

2 quarts (1.9 liters) chicken stock

2 bay leaves

6 peppercorns

1/4 teaspoon (1.25 milliliters) whole thyme

salt and pepper, to taste

1 pound (454 grams) puff pastry dough

3 cups (720 milliliters) grated Swiss cheese

2 eggs

Slice the onions very thinly and sauté them in butter in a skillet, stirring constantly, until a golden brown. Add the chicken stock. Wrap the spices in cheesecloth and add to the soup, then cook for 30-45 minutes. Season the soup with salt and pepper.

Have 6 soup cups ready. Roll out the dough and cut 6 circles slightly larger than the tops of the soup cups.

Using half the Swiss cheese, divide it into the 6 cups, then fill the rest of each cup with onion soup. Brush the top (outside) of the cup with egg, place the dough circle on top, and seal around the cup. Brush the dough with the rest of the egg and sprinkle the rest of the cheese over it.

Bake the soup in a hot (375°) oven for 5-6 minutes or until the dough puffs up and is golden brown.

Serves: 6

Jean Leon's **La Scala** in Beverly Hills has been a consistent favorite among Southern California gourmet diners for almost 25 years.

Leon came to the United States from the Basque country of France in 1951. After two years in the army, he made plans to open a restaurant in partnership with actor and friend James Dean. Dean was killed just two days before the deal was to go into escrow, and Leon had to temporarily abandon his plans and continue his job as a waiter. At that time he was also driving a cab to help raise the money he would need to open his own restaurant.

Late in 1956, La Scala was opened on the site of 11 previous restaurant failures. For a while it appeared La Scala would be number 12. But then the movie colony discovered the authentic Northern Italian cuisine of Emilio Nunez.

Mr. Nunez has been at La Scala since 1957. He was trained as a saucier at The Palace Hotel in Venice. His creations, such as Fettucine Leon, have earned him a loyal following. Every year Mr. Nunez and Mr. Leon make a "gastronomic tour" of Southern France and Northern Italy.

In the 1950s Leon and Nunez designed an enormous wine cellar that today houses one of the most extensive imported and domestic collections in the country.

La Scala plays host to innumerable celebrities; the famous know that at Mr. Leon's restaurant, they are assured of their privacy. And while the La Scala dining room is elegant, it is also casual.

La Scala is open weekdays for lunch and dinner and Saturdays for dinner only. All major credit cards are honored. Prices are moderately expensive to expensive.

La Scala

9455 Santa Monica Boulevard
Beverly Hills, California
(213) 275-0579

Proprietor: Jean Leon
Chef: Emilio Nunez

SCALOPPINI DI VITELLO TARTUFATTO

1 pound (454 grams) veal, cut in 12 thin slices about 1/8-inch (.32-centimeter) thick

salt and pepper, to taste

1/4 cup (60 milliliters) all-purpose flour

6 tablespoons (90 milliliters) clarified butter

1 tablespoon (15 milliliters) chopped shallots

1/2 cup (120 milliliters) Madeira wine

2 tablespoons (30 milliliters) all-purpose flour

1/4 cup (60 milliliters) whipping cream

3/4 cup (180 milliliters) beef broth

chopped truffles (optional)

Sprinkle the veal with salt and pepper and dip in the 1/4 cup (60 milliliters) flour. In a large skillet, heat 2/3 of the butter. When the butter is hot, add the veal, half at a time, and brown quickly on both sides. Arrange the veal on a serving platter and keep warm.

In the same skillet, cook the shallots in the remaining butter. Remove from heat and allow the pan to cool slightly. Add the Madeira and flame. When the flame is extinguished, blend the remaining flour, cream, and broth together and add to the skillet. Strain.

Serve the strained sauce over the veal slices, sprinkled with chopped truffles, if desired.

Serves: 6

Wine: *Nozzole*

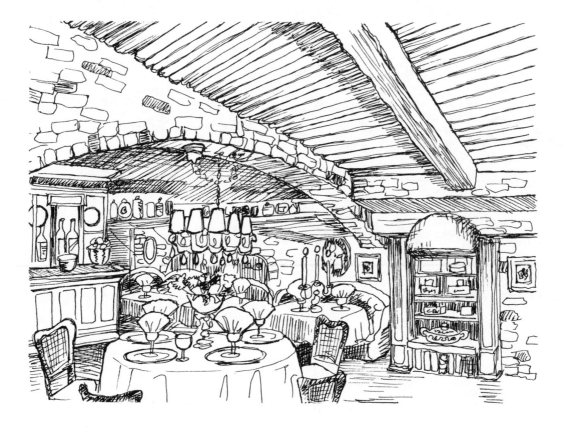

Cellar Restaurant is an eleven-year-old, award-winning French restaurant featuring classic cuisine as well as experimental dishes. It is located about four miles north of Disneyland, in the basement of an old hotel called Villa Del Sol. The decor is both rustic and elegant and certainly romantic—a mixture of splashing fountains, bright fresh flowers, tree ferns, soft candlelight, imported china, huge wine glasses, fine table linens, and wine-making artifacts—all enclosed by a secluded patio and a series of warm, cozy dining areas.

Proprietor Louis Schnelli was born into a restaurant family and raised in Switzerland. His considerable experience includes tenures in many European hotel kitchens and as manager of the Swiss Pavilion at Expo '67 in Montreal. Chef Salvatore Troia is Italian-born, was trained in Europe, and joined the Cellar in 1974. He went on to win the pres-tigious Chef of the Year award presented by the Southern California Restaurant Writers.

The Cellar opened in 1970 as a traditional French restaurant but has since altered its menu to include other adventuresome and creative cuisine. Messrs. Schnelli and Troia spend their vacations in Europe sampling some of the best *nouvelle cuisine* and then return to adapt them to their own and their customers' tastes. The restaurant also features a wine list of 400 labels, both imported and domestic, ranging in price from $6 to $250, and also offers superb home-made pastries for dessert. You will enjoy the experienced, attentive service provided during your meal.

Cellar Restaurant is open for dinner, Tuesday through Saturday. Seating is limited to 90, so reservations are essential. Jackets are required for men; all major credit cards are accepted. Prices are moderately expensive.

Cellar Restaurant

305 North Harbor Boulevard
Fullerton, California 92632
(714) 525-5682

Proprietor: Louis Schnelli
Chef: Salvatore Troia

ASPARAGUS NOUVELLE

2 pounds (.9 kilograms) fresh asparagus, peeled and trimmed to 4 inches (10 centimeters)

boiling water, as needed

pinch of salt

6 medium-sized leaves of Boston lettuce

3 Belgian endives, trimmed and julienne

1 celery root, trimmed and julienne

12 ounces (360 milliliters) Marukkan Dressing (recipe follows)

3/4 teaspoon (3.75 milliliters) herb mixture of freshly chopped tarragon, basil, chives, and thyme

2 medium-sized eggs, boiled 9 minutes, peeled and diced small

Boil the asparagus for 1 minute only. Add salt, chill quickly, and remove from water until ready to use.

Place the lettuce leaves over the julienne of Belgian endive and celery root on a warm salad plate.

In a saucepan, heat the asparagus with Marukkan Dressing and fresh herbs for no longer than 5 seconds after the boiling point is reached. Place the asparagus over the other ingredients on the salad plate, add diced boiled eggs and remaining dressing, and serve immediately.

Marukkan Dressing

2 ounces (56 grams) shallots, freshly chopped

1 1/2 ounces (45 milliliters) Kadoya brown sesame oil

7 ounces (210 milliliters) light sesame oil

9 ounces (270 milliliters) Marukkan seasoned vinegar

1 ounce (30 milliliters) white wine vinegar

1/2 ounce (15 milliliters) imported Dijon mustard

In a saucepan, lightly sauté the chopped shallots with some of the sesame oil dressing. Add the remaining ingredients and mix well with a wire whip.

Serves: 6

Hugo's V

Hyatt Regency Los Angeles
711 Hope Street
Los Angeles, California
(213) 683-1234

Hugo's V at the Hyatt Regency Los Angeles is justifiably proud of its recent acquisition of Executive Chef Roger Gustavson. A 1964 graduate of the Culinary Institute, he has been employed by the Waldorf Astoria Hotel and La Caravelle Restaurant in New York City, the Paris Hilton, the M.G.M. Grand Hotel in Las Vegas, the Royal Viking Lines, and most recently, the Hyatt Corporation. Many of the Hugo's restaurants (located in Hyatt Regency Hotels around the country) can be considered to be among our finest. The Los Angeles Hugo's belongs to that group.

Hugo's serves gourmet Continental food in a traditional, elegant atmosphere. It is unusual to find an ambiance so intimate and unhurried in the restaurants of deluxe hotels, but at Hugo's V, the top priority of the staff is to insure that the diner never feels rushed.

A Hugo's specialty is the Spinach Salad. It's an impressive presentation of crisp spinach, mushrooms, eggs, peeled tomatoes, smoked almonds, and freshly prepared pepper dressing. Their entrées are classic French and Continental preparations.

Hugo's V serves lunch and dinner Monday through Friday from 11:30 a.m. until 2:30 p.m. and from 6:00 p.m. until 11:00 p.m. The restaurant is not usually open on weekends. Phone ahead for a reservation and dress formally. All major credit cards are accepted. Prices are moderately expensive.

FRESH CREAM OF RASPBERRY SOUP

2 cups (480 milliliters) chicken stock

2 pints (.95 liter) fresh raspberries

1/2 cup (120 milliliters) sour cream

1 cup (240 milliliters) corn syrup

1/4 cup (60 milliliters) sugar

2 fresh limes

4 ounces (120 milliliters) framboise liqueur

In a blender, combine all the ingredients. Blend on low speed for about 30 seconds. Serve well chilled in cold glass bowls with a spoonful of unsweetened whipped cream and a fresh raspberry on top.

Serves: 4

Proprietor Ali Rabbani paints an exotic profile of his **Marrakesh** restaurant: "As you step in the door you will have flown over the Atlantic to the Arabian Desert where you will be invited to a Sheik's caravan on a moonlit night. In a rich tent, you will be seated in an atmosphere of Moroccan hospitality."

Mr. Rabbani's syntax is colorful, but he does not exaggerate. Marrakesh is an unusual dining experience. You sit in opulent canvas tents on divans and plump pillows. Oriental rugs, potted palms, and mosaic floors characterize the North African decor. A tableside hand washing ritual precedes the authentic cuisine which you eat without knives or forks. Mr. Rabbani opened Marrakesh five years ago and has employed the same Moroccan chef over that time. You can be sure of enjoying gourmet, yet home-cooked style Moroccan cuisine whenever you dine at Marrakesh.

An awesome venture is their eight course feast which is highlighted by entrées of chicken, fish, rabbit, or quail. The quail is roasted and served with rice, raisins, and almonds. The rabbit is baked in garlic sauce and set in prunes and sesame seeds.

The Marrakesh wine list offers both domestic and imported vintages, but a Moroccan or Algerian wine is recommended for a genuine North African evening. There is full bar service and capuccino is served as well.

Dress is casual and all major credit cards are accepted. Marrakesh is open seven days for dinner only. Prices are moderately expensive.

Marrakesh

100 West Pacific Coast Highway
Newport Beach, California 92663
(714) 645-8384

Proprietor: Ali Rabbani

CHICKEN "MQUALLI" WITH PICKLED LEMON

2 3-pound (1.35-kilogram) chickens

salt, to taste

4 ounces (120 milliliters) groundnut oil

1 tablespoon (15 milliliters) olive oil

2 ounces (60 milliliters) butter

1 heaping teaspoon (6 milliliters) ginger

1 small whole onion

2-3 cloves crushed garlic

1 teaspoon (5 milliliters) saffron

2 cups (480 milliliters) water, or as needed

10 preserved olives

zest of 1 pickled lemon cut in quarters

Put the chickens, whole or cut into pieces, with their fat and offal, in a thick-bottomed sauce-pan. Add the salt, oils, butter, ginger, onion, garlic, saffron, and water. Cover and heat until it comes to a boil, then turn the chicken pieces over, stir to mix the spices, and let cook on moderate heat. Make sure the sauce does not boil away and add a little water if necessary. Turn the pieces frequently so the chickens are completely impregnated with sauce. Remove the onion as soon as it is cooked and set aside.

When the chickens are cooked (the flesh comes away from the bones easily), remove them to a serving dish. Add the olives and lemon zest to the sauce and allow to simmer for a few minutes.

Take a little piece of the chicken liver and the reserved onion and either sieve or blend in an electric mixer, then add to the sauce. Bring the sauce to a boil. Stir the sauce with a hard circular movement, then pour it over the chicken and serve immediately. Suggestion: serve with saffron rice or noodles.

Serves: 4

Wine: *Dry, white wine*

There have been several recent changes in management, decor, and menu at the elegant **Chez Cary**, but be assured that the essential traditions of superlative Continental cuisine and exemplary service have been maintained. Sean Lewis may be new as Manager, but he's been with the restaurant for many years.

An evening at Chez Cary begins with attentive valet parking service. Inside, your table is set with heavy silver and delicate crystal. You will be helped into red velvet winged swivel chairs as a violinist strolls nearby. Enjoy a cocktail while you plan your meal and wine selections. (There are over 700 imported and domestic wines to choose from.) Among several fine entrées created by

Executive Chef Klaus Dornen is the Veal Chez Cary (loin of veal with white asparagus topped with Hollandaise and Westphalian ham presented on a Sauce Bordelaise bed). Duck à l'Apricot is another favorite, as is Scampis Glacé Comtesse. And desserts are special, too, at Chez Cary. The Soufflé Amaretto is just one exotic and delicious way to close out your meal. You will find your car waiting at the door, motor running, when it is time to leave.

Chez Cary is open seven days for dinner only from 6:30 p.m. to 10:00 p.m. Monday through Friday and Sunday, 5:30 p.m. to 10:00 p.m. Saturday. Call for a reservation and dress formally. All major credit cards are honored. Prices are expensive.

Chez Cary

571 South Main Street
Orange, California 92668
(714) 542-3595   Manager: Sean Lewis

SCAMPIS GLACÉ COMTESSE
(Casserole of Shrimp in Creamed Sherry Sauce)

12 jumbo shrimp

1 teaspoon (5 milliliters) sweet butter

1 teaspoon (5 milliliters) chopped garlic

1 teaspoon (5 milliliters) chopped shallots

dash of salt

dash of white pepper

1/2 cup (120 milliliters) dry sherry

1/2 cup (120 milliliters) dry white wine

dash of Lea & Perrins Worcestershire sauce

1 tablespoon (15 milliliters) roux

3 egg yolks

1 cup (240 milliliters) whipped cream

Peel the shrimp and split them lengthwise. Place the shrimp, butter, garlic, shallots, salt, pepper, sherry, white wine, and Worcestershire sauce in a saucepan, cover, and bring to a boil. Boil approximately 3 minutes. Remove the shrimp and place them in ovenproof dishes.

Bring the remaining mixture back to a boil, then strain into a clean pan. Add roux and boil for another 3 minutes, stirring with a whip. Remove the pan from the heat and stir in the egg yolks, then the whipped cream, to make a smooth sauce.

Cover the shrimp with the sauce and brown under the broiler. Serve as an appetizer.

Serves: 6

Vinchenzo's

Chef: Keith Garton

901 East Del Mar
Pasadena, California 91106
(213) 795-8823

Vinchenzo's is a two-year-old restaurant located in the charming old community of Pasadena—a short drive from downtown Los Angeles. It is owned by Jerry Hultgren who has been in the restaurant business since he was a teenager and whose experience includes exposure to nearly all facets of the food service industry—primarily under the auspices of the Sheraton organization. His restaurant, Vinchenzo's, is charming and comfortable. It only seats 80, so it's also intimate. The decor is characterized by warm plum colors, white linen, silver place settings, and private booths.

The menu displays a wide variety of traditional American and Continental dishes, as well as the personal creations of Chef Keith Garton, and includes Seafood Stuffed Mushrooms or Scampi Vinchenzo's to start, followed by Potage le Onion or a special soup de jour, then a seafood salad or a cobb salad for two. Some of the more interesting entrées are the Veal Zurich, the Fillet of Sand Dabs, and the Chicken Wellington. Follow your entrée with a dessert such as Burnt Creme or Bananas George or Amaretto Mousse Pie or a selection from the pastry cart that changes selections each day and you have had a memorable meal.

I must also mention the lunch menu because it's about as big as the dinner menu. In addition to the wide variety of choices always available, two daily luncheon specials are also offered. The wine cellar is well-stocked with moderately priced selections from France and Italy and, interestingly, small California vintners, some of whom make the best wine in the country.

Vinchenzo's is open for lunch, Monday through Friday, and for dinner, Tuesday through Saturday. Reservations are essential due to the limited seating capacity. Dress is casual and most major credit cards are accepted. Prices are moderate.

VEAL ZURICH

4 ounces (120 milliliters) clarified butter

24 ounces (672 grams) top round or better veal, julienne

flour, to dust

2 teaspoons (10 milliliters) chopped shallots

8 ounces (224 grams) sliced mushrooms

1 tablespoon (15 milliliters) flour

16 ounces (480 milliliters) heavy cream, warmed

1 tablespoon (15 milliliters) paprika

salt, to taste

Heat the butter in a sauté pan. Dust the veal in flour and add to the butter when it is hot enough to sear the meat. Working quickly, so as not to overcook the veal, sear all the meat then remove it to a heatproof casserole and keep warm.

In the same sauté pan, add the shallots, mushrooms, and the 1 tablespoon (15 milliliters) flour. Sauté until a very light brown roux is formed. Stir warm cream into the roux and cook until reduced to a thick sauce (approximately 8 minutes over medium heat). Add paprika and salt, then pour the sauce over the veal. Suggestion: serve with buttered noodles sprinkled with poppy seeds and garnished with parsley.

Serves: 4

Wine: *Vouvray*

Aldo's Restaurant's Chef/Co-Owner Paul Coulat supervises the preparation of over 50 Continental dishes. A Master Chef of wide experience in Europe and South America, Mr. Coulat has spent the last 15 years at Aldo's in Sacramento in association with Host/Co-Owner Aldo Bovero. The dining room is charming: brick walls, reds and purples, wine bins, and fresh flowers create the atmosphere for an enjoyable respite from the action outside. There is a pleasant bar, and a versatile pianist plays for genuine easy listening.

Aldo's menu is almost overwhelming. You may order any one of their Continental dishes, say the Beef Wellington or boneless Trout Sauté Belle Meunière or Fettuccine Romana, and it will be true to the classic preparation. Of course there are dishes unique to Aldo's: Duckling in Terrine, Tournedos Champignons à la Paul, and a sirloin and stuffed quail combination. And there's the incomparable Lamb Gourmande. It's a loin of lamb sautéed with shallots, brandy, Perigourdine Sauce, and Pâté of Goose Liver wrapped in puff pastry and served with wild rice and asparagus Hollandaise. Aldo's wine list features over 100 quality selections.

Dress is neat and all credit cards are honored at Aldo's. Open six days for lunch and dinner, be sure to phone for a reservation as seating is limited. Prices are moderately expensive.

Aldo's Restaurant

2914 Pasatiempo Lane
Town and Country Village
Sacramento, California 95812
(916) 483-5031

Proprietors:
Aldo Bovero and Paul Coulat
Chef: Paul Coulat

PEAR FLAMBÉ ALDO

6 teaspoons (30 milliliters) sugar

4 tablespoons (60 milliliters) butter

8 pear halves stuck with cloves

2 ounces (60 milliliters) triple sec

1 pint (470 milliliters) chocolate syrup

4 scoops vanilla ice cream

In a flambé pan, caramelize the sugar. Add the butter and pear halves and cook for 3 minutes. Pour in the triple sec and flame. Add the chocolate syrup and cook for an additional 5 minutes. Serve over vanilla ice cream.

Serves: 4

Wine: *Sauterne, Chateau Saudirot, or Asti Spumante*

El Bizcocho Restaurant

Chef: Jacques Cornelis

Rancho Bernardo Inn
17550 Bernardo Oaks Drive
San Diego, California 092128
(714) 487-1611

El Bizcocho Restaurant is the main dining room of the picturesque and prestigious Rancho Bernardo Inn. Rancho Bernardo is a relatively new, planned community—a part of San Diego city located about 35 miles northeast of downtown—that, because of its location and climate, is quickly becoming the retirement home of the wealthy as well as *the* place to live while on the way up. The Rancho Bernardo Inn, built in 1963, is the hub of a series of championship golf courses and other recreational facilities, all of which weave through the properties of many of the areas fine homes.

The restaurant itself is four years old and is reminiscent of a dining room in a turn-of-the-century luxury resort. The view overlooks one of the golf courses and out to a sprawling valley surrounded by manicured residential hillsides. Inside, you become immediately aware of the cordiality and intimacy of the Spanish architecture and furnishings—stone walls, beamed ceilings, archways, paned glass windows, and comfortable high-backed chairs are tastefully combined.

The menu reveals an extensive array of traditional French dishes augmented by specialties that feature local seafood. The house specialty is an excellent Saumon en Papillote, which is salmon delicately steamed inside parchment. I consider the Boeuf à la Wellington and the Coquille St. Jacques aux Poireaux, among others, to be special as well. A call for dessert yields a rolling cart of delicacies ranging from rich chocolate mousse, fresh whipped cream, and strawberries to tortes and cakes of all descriptions. All of the food is delicious, the setting is most conducive to fine eating, and the service is excellent.

El Bizcocho Restaurant at the Rancho Bernardo Inn is open for luncheon buffet and dinner, seven days a week. Reservations are suggested; jackets are required for men at dinner. All major credit cards are welcome. Prices are moderately expensive.

SAUMON EN PAPILLOTE

4 ounces (112 grams) each of leeks, carrots, and celery, cut in 3-inch (8-centimeter) julienne strips

salted water, as needed

4 pieces parchment paper, 25 x 20 inches (64 x 51 centimeters)

4 8-ounce (224-gram) salmon fillets

salt and pepper, to taste

4 tablespoons (60 milliliters) butter

fresh tarragon leaves, to taste

4 tablespoons (60 milliliters) fish stock

cooking oil, as needed

Blanche the vegetables for 3 minutes in salted water. Grease half of each of the 4 pieces of paper. Divide half of the vegetables into 4 equal portions and place 1 portion each onto each piece of greased parchment paper, near the middle of the paper.

Season each salmon fillet with salt and pepper. Divide the remaining blanched vegetables into 4 equal portions and place on top of the salmon fillets. Place 1 tablespoon (15 milliliters) butter and fresh tarragon leaves on top of each fillet.

Pour 1 tablespoon (15 milliliters) fish stock over each fillet. Fold the paper over in the middle and close the ends tightly. Place the closed packets in a pan of smoking hot oil. Bake at 425° for approximately 10 minutes. Remove from oven, slice the paper open, and serve.

Serves: 4

Wine: *Davis Bynum Allen-Hafner Reserve Chardonnay, 1978*

Casina Valadier

Proprietor: Joseph Ferrari
Chef: Josette Ferrari

4445 Lamont Street
San Diego, California 92109
(714) 270-8650

You'll dine at **Casina Valadier** in a converted home surrounded by trees and shrubbery. There's a delightful outdoor patio, and the small indoor dining rooms exude an irresistible personal warmth. There are fresh flowers on each table and the coordination of the patterned apricot wallpaper and the sky-blue tablecloths is charming. Cocktails are accompanied by fried zucchini, and if your appetite needs whetting, no combination is more efficient.

The name Casina Valadier is borrowed from a Roman restaurant of the same name. It recalls the Italian architect of French origin commissioned by Napoleon to bring the Borghese Gardens to life again. In the persons of owners Giuseppe Ferrari and his French-born wife, Josette, the merging of French and Italian influences has also worked to positive effect. Mrs. Ferrari began cooking many years ago in the restaurant of her family in Auberge, France. Mr. Ferrari has long worked in fine restaurants in Europe, South America, and the United States.

The menu is strictly à la carte and features homemade pastas and veal preparations. There are poultry and seafood if you are so inclined, but frankly, the pastas are most impressive. Giuseppe's pasta sampler is an appetizer of Cappeletti (stuffed veal, salami, and spices), Tortelli (filled with spinach and ricotta cheese), and Fettuccini Alfredo. Veal Scallopini Valdostanda is with mushrooms, Prosciutto, and Fontina cheese. Your waiter or Mr. Ferrari will appraise you of that particular evening's desserts. Do try the Amaretto Mousse or the Ricotta Amaretto Cream Pie if they're offered that night; they are superb and unique.

Casina Valadier is open for dinner Tuesday through Saturday; reservations are recommended as is formal wear. All major credit cards are honored. Prices are moderately expensive.

RICOTTA AMARETTO CREAM PIE

1 cup (240 milliliters) graham
cracker crumbs

1/4 cup (60 milliliters) melted butter

2 tablespoons (30 milliliters) sugar

1 cup (240 milliliters) chopped
almonds

2 1/2 cups (600 milliliters) ricotta
cheese

1/2 cup (120 milliliters) sugar

2 ounces (56 grams) sweet
chocolate, chopped

2 ounces (60 milliliters) Amaretto
liqueur

1 ounce (30 milliliters) Kahlua
liqueur

3/4 cup (180 milliliters) heavy cream,
whipped

2 ounces (56 grams) sweet
chocolate, shaved

To prepare the crust: combine the cracker
crumbs, melted butter, and 2 tablespoons (30
milliliters) sugar and press firmly onto the
bottom of a 9-inch (23-centimeter) spring form
pan. Bake for 5 minutes at 375°. Cool.

Roast the almonds until a light golden brown.
Cool.

Beat the ricotta cheese and the remaining
sugar together, then mix in 3/4 of the roasted
almonds, the chopped chocolate, and the
Amaretto and Kahlua. Then fold in the
whipped cream. Pour and spread this mixture
over the crust, then sprinkle the remaining
almonds and the shaved chocolate onto the pie.
Refrigerate for at least 6 hours before serving.

Serves: 12

Wine: *Asti Spumante*

Dining at **Mister A's** atop the Fifth Avenue Financial Center is a special pleasure because, in addition to an award winning menu, the accompanying panoramic view of San Diego, the Bay, and Mexico is spectacular. The Continental atmosphere—candelabras, chandeliers, wine bins, and Renaissance paintings—create a comfortable ambiance, and a circular bar and cocktail lounge add to the congeniality.

Dominic J. Alessio has been associated with Mister A's since its opening 15 years ago. The pride of the house is a special Beef Wellington (tenderloin with duxelles of mushrooms, foie gras, pâté Feuilleté, sauce Perigueux) served with soufflé potatoes. The Long Island Duckling au Grand Marnier and Médallions of Veal Normande are recommended diversions from the principal Mister A's preparation: beef. Grenadins of Beef Chasseur is tenderloin in Marsala wine, mushrooms and tarragon. The Chateaubriand with Sauce Béarnaise is a prime filet prepared to order.

The house wine is Louis Martini by the glass, Macon Villages if you'd prefer a bottle. There is also an impressive wine list: most domestic and European regions are represented.

Mister A's is open seven days: Monday through Friday for lunch, 11:30 a.m. to 3:00 p.m., and dinner, 6:00 p.m. to 10:30 p.m.; Saturday and Sunday for dinner only. Dress is formal and always call ahead to reserve a table. All major credit cards are accepted. Prices are moderately expensive.

Mister A's

2550 Fifth Avenue
San Diego, California 92103
(714) 239-1377

Proprietor: Dominic J. Alessio
Chef: David Segal

MISTER A'S SPECIAL BEEF WELLINGTON

1 1/2 pounds (681 grams) bread flour

1/2 teaspoon (2.5 milliliters) salt

6 ounces (168 grams) butter

6 ounces (168 grams) shortening

3 egg yolks

1 teaspoon (5 milliliters) olive oil

3/4-1 cup (180-240 milliliters) cold water

5 pounds (2.25 kilograms) beef tenderloin, whole trimmed and peeled

8 ounces (224 grams) liver pâté or foie gras

finely chopped truffle peelings, as needed

1 egg, beaten

To prepare pâté en croûte: sift the flour, then fold into it the salt, butter, shortening, egg yolks, olive oil, and cold water as for pie dough. Blend together lightly. Cover the dough with a cloth and allow to stand for one hour.

Sear the tenderloin well, leaving the center practically raw. Cool the tenderloin and spread with liver pâté or foie gras. Sprinkle with chopped truffles.

Roll out the pâté en croûte dough to 3/16-inch (.5-centimeter) thick. Wrap the dough around the tenderloin, keeping the seam on the bottom. Fold the ends under. Brush with beaten egg and place on an oiled baking sheet. Bake in a 375° oven for approximately 40 minutes or until done. (If the dough browns too quickly, shield it with foil.)

Cut the Wellington into slices about 3/4-inch (2-centimeters) thick. Suggestion: serve with Madeira or poivrade sauce.

Serves: 8

Wine: *Red Bordeaux*

Once a speakeasy called the Philosophers Inn, the **Blue Fox Restaurant** is now a fine Continental restaurant featuring northern Italian and French cuisine. It is a large restaurant with three main dining salons and three private party rooms. The main rooms are decorated in gold, red, and white accented by gold leaf Ionic columns, imported crystal chandeliers, and plush carpeting. The food is served from antique Georgian and English silver pieces, and the walls are covered with reproductions of well-known 19th century paintings. The Large Wine Cellar, one of the three private dining salons, has similar plush red carpeting and high-backed chairs and also features 16th century Italian furniture all hand-carved by one family. The walls of another room, the Original Wine Cellar, are lined with over 300 varieties of fine wines imported from all over the world.

Owner Mario Mondin comes from a family of restaurateurs and began his own career upon arriving in America from Italy at age 17. He then worked in all phases of the restaurant business until 1942 when he purchased the Blue Fox.

His menu offers a wide variety of traditional favorites as well as several unique items whose recipes were brought to America by Mr. Mondin's two grandmothers. (One such recipe appears on the opposite page.)

Prix fixe five-course dinners are served before 7:30 p.m. These are excellent values, featuring a choice of seven entrées, including Filet de Boeuf Stroganoff, Veal Scaloppine Marsala, and Fillets of Sole-meunière—all expertly prepared by Chef Walter Sturzenegger.

The Blue Fox Restaurant is open for dinner, Monday through Saturday. Jackets and ties are required, as are reservations. All major credit cards are welcome. Prices are moderately expensive.

Blue Fox Restaurant

659 Merchant Street
San Francisco, California 94111
(415) 981-1177

Proprietor: Mario Mondin
Chef: Walter Sturzenegger

VEAL TONNE

1 1/2 pounds (681 grams) veal, trimmed of fat, nerves, and sinew

3 quarts (2.8 liters) water, or more as needed

3 branches celery

1 medium onion

1 medium carrot

4 cloves

2 ounces (60 milliliters) vinegar

salt, to taste

Tonne Sauce (*recipe follows*)

capers, to decorate

Place veal in cheesecloth and roll into the shape of a sausage. Fasten both ends with string and also make three ties in between. Place tied veal in a pot with water, celery, onion, carrot, cloves, vinegar, and salt. Bring to a boil and let simmer for 1 1/2 hours, covered. Add more water if necessary. Remove the veal from the pot and place under a weight to extract moisture. Let stand until cool, then place in refrigerator until firm. Do not remove cloth until ready to serve.

Remove cheesecloth and string. Cut the veal into thin slices and arrange them on a platter in an overlapping pattern. Pour Tonne Sauce over it and decorate with capers. (Optional: also decorate with pieces of gherkins, sliced olives, sliced hard-boiled eggs, etc.)

Tonne Sauce

2 stalks celery

1 small green onion

2 teaspoons (10 milliliters) capers

1 7-ounce (196-gram) can tuna in olive oil

6 fillets of anchovies

1 quart (950 milliliters) homemade mayonnaise

2 ounces (60 milliliters) lemon juice

dash of Tabasco sauce

salt, to taste

Put the first 5 ingredients through a food grinder and make a fine purée. Add mayonnaise, lemon juice, and Tabasco. Mix until well blended. Salt to taste.

Wine: *California Chardonnay or imported Meursault*

Serves: 8

La Bourgogne Restaurant

Proprietor: Jean Lapuyade
Chef: Louis Marticorena

330 Mason Street
San Francisco, California 94102
(415) 362-7352

Jean Lapuyade opened **La Bourgogne Restaurant** 20 years ago. His formula for success was simple: establish elegance in decor and menu, let diners feel relaxed, and serve original provincial French food carefully prepared by meticulous chefs.

The dining room is reminiscent of a grand hall in an ocean liner. Walls are draped in silver and gold silk, chandeliers are reflected in mirrored columns, booths are plush and intimate, and there are long tables with fresh roses and silver flawlessly set upon them.

At La Bourgogne every entrée is interesting. Dover Sole Chambertin is a glazed sole in red wine sauce. Croûte de Homard Brillat Savarin is a pastry crust filled with medallions of lobster and thin zucchini in a lobster sauce

with a hint of curry. (The pastry is topped with Hollandaise immediately prior to serving.) Another specialty is the Filet de Boeuf en croûte à la Moede de Mivernais (marinated hearts of filet of beef surrounded by pâté foie gras in pastry, and topped with mushrooms and wine sauce). Soufflé Grand Marnier is their special dessert. The wine list offers an extensive collection of imported and domestic vintages, and chilled cocktails will be prepared on request.

Be sure to make reservations as seating in this exclusive restaurant is always at a premium. La Bourgogne is open six days a week for dinner only. Formal wear is required and all major credit cards are accepted. Prices are expensive.

DOVER SOLE CHAMBERTIN

16 ounces (454 grams) Dover sole

**1/2 pint (240 milliliters) red wine,
Chambertin preferred**

2 chopped shallots

1/2 cup (120 milliliters) demi-glaze

5 ounces (150 milliliters) butter

1 tablespoon (15 milliliters) flour

Poach the Dover sole in the wine with the chopped shallots. Strain and reduce the liquid to half, then boil with the demi-glaze. Thicken this sauce with a lump of butter kneaded with the flour. Boil, remove from heat, and stir in the rest of the butter.

Arrange the sole on a long silver dish, cover with sauce, and glaze quickly in the broiler.

Serves: 2

Doros, located in what was formerly the legendary Barbary Coast, has contributed to San Francisco's international reputation for fine dining since it was first opened more than 25 years ago.

The essential ingredients of this award-winning restaurant are Don A. Dianda, a stellar restaurateur who is an honorary Director of the National Restaurant Association, and Executive Chef Paul Bermani. For over 40 years Bermani has been successfully preparing virtually every classical cuisine.

The Doros menu ranges from the Russian Breast of Chicken à la Kiev to the French Medallion of Beef Tenderloin Pompadour to the Italian Saltimbocca à la Romana with Risotto. They also prepare uniquely American dishes—the Lobster Tail and Filet

Mignon combination, for example. "Nevertheless," says Mr. Dianda, "if a guest comes in and asks for a dish which is not on our menu at the moment, we will make it for him."

The Doros decor is elegant and simple, in the best sense of the words. The service is attentive, not obtrusive. The wine cellar is stocked with fine imported and domestic wines, liqueurs, and champagnes. And you can have a cocktail if you like.

Doros is open six days a week, 11:30 a.m. to 2:30 p.m. for weekday lunch; 6:00 p.m. to 10:30 p.m. Monday through Saturday for dinner. Reservations are a must, and formal dress is required. All major credit cards are honored. Prices are expensive.

Doros

714 Montgomery Street
San Francisco, California 94111
(415) 397-6822

Proprietor: Don A. Dianda
Executive Chef: Paul Bermani

VEAL SCALOPPINE PICCATA

12 thin slices veal loin, pounded flat

salt and pepper, to taste

flour, to dust

1 cup (240 milliliters) butter

1/4 cup (60 milliliters) dry sauterne wine

juice of 1 lemon

1/2 cup (120 milliliters) brown sauce, prepared

1 tablespoon (15 milliliters) capers

1 tablespoon (15 milliliters) chopped green onions

2 tablespoons (30 milliliters) solid butter

Season the veal with salt and pepper, then dip in flour to cover both sides lightly. Melt the cup of butter (240 milliliters) in a large skillet, then add the veal slices to it when the butter bubbles. When the veal is browned on both sides, pour off the excess butter. Pour in the wine and instantly light it with a match. When the flame burns out, simmer for 3 minutes. Add the lemon juice and brown sauce to the pan. When the mixture is bubbling, pour a little of the sauce onto a warm serving platter and arrange the veal slices on top.

To the rest of the sauce remaining in the skillet, add the capers, green onion, and 2 tablespoons (30 milliliters) solid butter. Shake the skillet to swirl and melt the butter, then pour the sauce over the veal. Serve immediately.

Serves: 4

Fournou's Ovens

Proprietor: James A. Nassikas
Chef: Marcel Dragon

Stanford Court Hotel
905 California Street
San Francisco, California 94108
(415) 989-1910

Late in 1968, The Stanford Court Hotel spent nearly $1 million to build an unusual extension to its original restaurant, **Fournou's Ovens**. The idea to design the restaurant like a Victorian conservatory was to create an atmosphere suited to people's dining attitudes and comfort.

But it is exquisite to look at as well. Art nouveau in mood, the copper-roofed conservatories are designed to harmonize architecturally with the Italianate façade of the hotel. The design is based on the glass enclosed winter gardens popular in Europe during the early 1800s. The interior stucco walls are the original outer walls of the restored hotel itself. Adorning the interior walls are terra-cotta and limestone bas-relief panels from 19th century New York buildings.

Marcel Dragon supervises the Continental preparations at Fournou's. He began training at the age of 14 in Monte Carlo. He subsequently created meals aboard Prince Rainier's private yacht. He has been at the Stanford Court since 1972.

Fournou's Ovens is famous for its open-hearth oven preparations such as the Roast Rack of Lamb with Sauce aux Aromates. An appetizer of Fresh Duck Liver in Terrine with Pistachios, a salad Niçoise, and one of nine gourmet desserts (such as Soufflé Glacé Grand Marnier) are all refreshingly authentic recommendations for dinner.

Fournou's Ovens is open for lunch and dinner Monday through Friday, reservations are recommended, and gentlemen should wear jackets and ties. Major credit cards are honored. Prices are moderately expensive.

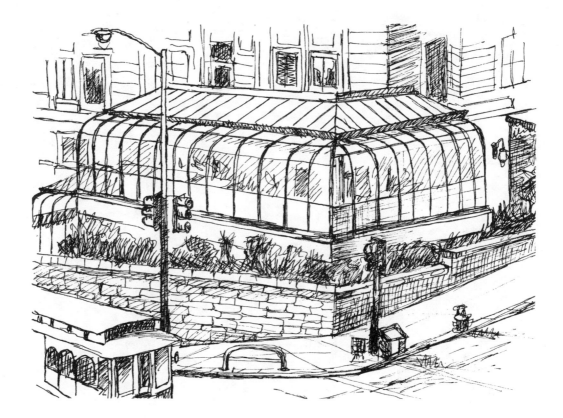

CRAB LEGS BERCY

3/4 cup (180 milliliters) dry white wine

1 teaspoon (5 milliliters) lemon juice

2 shallots, finely minced

6 tablespoons (90 milliliters) soft, sweet butter

1/2 cup (120 milliliters) fish demi-glaze

32 freshly cooked Dungeness crab legs

1 tablespoon (15 milliliters) freshly chopped parsley

salt and white pepper, to taste

Reduce the white wine and lemon juice in a sauté pan over high heat. Lower the heat and add the minced shallots. Then, add the soft butter, lump by lump. Swirl the pan constantly or stir with a light wire whisk to melt the butter without it separating (very important). Add the fish demi-glaze and continue to swirl or whisk. Add the crab legs and finish with parsley and salt and pepper.

Serves: 4

Hugo's One Up is located high above San Francisco's civic center district on the 36th floor of the magnificent Hyatt Hotel. This seven-year-old restaurant provides one of the most breathtaking views of the city in an atmosphere of warmth and sophistication. The two-story ceiling is covered with striped satin latern cloth, and there are fascinating chandeliers, *Ficus benjaminus*, freshly cut flowers, contemporary furnishings, live piano music, and most of all, fine dinner fare.

Executive Chef Horst Boehler has been in the food service business for almost 30 years. Prior to joining the Hyatt organization, Chef Boehler worked extensively in restaurants and hotels throughout Europe. He has designated Hugo's One Up as a Continental restaurant, but the emphasis is on traditional French cuisine with some *nouvelle* offered.

Their most popular dishes are the house specialty, Steak Diane; an excellent rack of spring lamb; an unusual duckling recipe prepared by rubbing the bird with anise, orange zest, and fennel; a fine Beef Wellington; and Escalope de Veau Alsace.

The extensive list of imported and domestic wines supplement the house wine from Robert Mondavi of California. The dessert list is also extensive and offers such delights as Russian creme, Grand Marnier, and Dutch chocolate soufflés, and an old favorite, Cherries Jubilee — to name just a few.

Hugo's One Up is open for lunch, Monday through Friday, and for dinner, seven nights a week. There is also a Sunday brunch. Call for reservations. Jackets and ties are specified, and all major credit cards are accepted. Prices are moderately expensive.

Hugo's One Up

Hyatt on Union Square
345 Stockton Street
San Francisco, California 94108
(415) 398-1234

Proprietor: Hyatt on Union Square
Chef: Horst Boehler

ESCALOPE DE VEAU ALSACE

1 6-ounce (168-gram) veal steak

2 ounces (56 grams) truffled goose liver pâté

salt, white pepper, and thyme, to taste

flour, to dust

2 tablespoons (30 milliliters) clarified butter

1/4 cup (60 milliliters) veal stock

1 ounce (30 milliliters) cognac

1/4 cup (60 milliliters) fresh heavy cream

Cut a pocket into the veal and stuff with the truffled goose liver pâté. Season with salt, pepper, and thyme. Slightly flour the veal, then sauté it in clarified butter. Remove the veal from the sauté pan.

Add the veal stock, cognac, and fresh cream to the sauté pan and stir over low heat until thick. Season this sauce with salt and pepper, then pour the sauce over the veal steak and serve.

Serves: 1

the Iron Horse

19 Maiden Lane
San Francisco, California 94108
(415) 362-8133

Proprietor: John J. Kukulica, Jr.

The Iron Horse is located on historic Maiden Lane Promenade — a two-block area of San Francisco that was a hotbed of cheap saloons and brothels at the end of the 19th century. In fact, this area had such a tough reputation, it was said to make the infamous Barbary Coast district by the waterfront seem very civilized. In 1906, however, everything changed. The earthquake destroyed Maiden Lane and cleared the way for massive renovation. The rebuilding brought a host of honest, small business people to the area, all hoping to establish a new, prosperous neighborhood. As time went on, their hopes became reality. In 1921, Fred Solari and Max David opened a restaurant which became the world famous Solaris. In 1955, the name was changed to The Iron Horse. In 1979, a former vice-president of a large catering firm, John Kukulica, Jr., took over the ownership, but in all the years, the place has remained the same warm gathering spot for discerning diners.

The Iron Horse seats only 80 people at a time. It is softly lit and has elegant table settings and piano music in the background. The excellent Continental cuisine and broiler items are prepared by Italian-born chef Roger Bertola who, at one time, owned his own restaurant in San Francisco's financial district. All of the veal dishes on the menu have been specially created by him. The rack of lamb is also a special treat. Imported and domestic wines at all price levels are available.

The Iron Horse is open for lunch and dinner, Monday through Saturday. Reservations are suggested. The dress code requires jackets for gentlemen, and all major credit cards are accepted. Prices are moderate.

MEDALLION OF VEAL RUGGERO

3 ounces (54 grams) mushrooms, pounded thin

6 teaspoons (30 milliliters) butter

6 ounces (168 grams) veal loin, pounded thin

1 ounce (30 milliliters) white wine

1/2 teaspoon (2.5 milliliters) lemon juice

salt and pepper, to taste

Sauté the mushrooms in 1/3 the butter. Sauté the veal in a separate preheated pan, over high heat, with 1/3 the butter. Brown both sides of the veal, then add wine and lemon juice. Add the remaining butter and season to taste. Shake the pan over the heat until the butter melts into a sauce consistency and serve with sautéed mushrooms on top.

Serves: 1

Wine: *Orvietto Dry Barberari, 1979*

Albion's serves a variety of elegant French entrées in a plush 1920s decor. Be prepared for an intimate and unhurried meal. You'll dine at a table set with fine crystal and silver, delicate china dishware, and a small vase of fresh flowers. Chandeliers and a San Francisco wooden bar with etched mirrors from the Roaring Twenties grace the dining room.

Proprietor Claude Gobet has been a chef for 21 years. Trained in France, he prepared entrées for Auberge de la Terrinée, an esteemed restaurant in his home country. At Albion's, the house speciality of lobster soufflé with red butter sauce, preceded by a pâté of salmon, whitefish, trout, and pistachios make for a very tasty and unusual seafood meal. Albion's also features chicken breasts in pastry with cherry sauce, sweetbreads with Meaux mustard, roasted rack of fresh lamb with thyme, filet mignon with grapes, and other equally ambitious French creations. Select an accompanying domestic or imported wine from Albion's extensive list and at least taste the Charlotte au Chocolat for dessert.

Albion's is open Monday through Friday for lunch from 11:30 to 2:30, for dinner Monday through Saturday 6:00 to 10:30. Call ahead to reserve a table and dress as you like, though remember, elegance is the word at Albion's. All major credit cards are accepted. Prices are moderately expensive.

Albion's

13422 Ventura Boulevard
Sherman Oaks, California 91423
(213) 981-6650

Proprietor/Chef: Claude Gobet

PÂTÉ DE POISSON AUX ASPERGES
(Hot Pâté of Sea Bass with Asparagus)

1 pound (454 grams) fillet of sea bass

1/4 cup (60 milliliters) dry white wine

2 1/2 teaspoons (12.5 milliliters) chopped shallots

1 tablespoon (15 milliliters) chopped tarragon

salt and freshly ground white pepper, to taste

2 egg whites

3/4 cup (180 milliliters) milk

1 dozen fresh asparagus

butter, as needed

1 teaspoon (5 milliliters) olive oil

3 medium-sized mushrooms, quartered

1 cup (240 milliliters) clam juice

3 tablespoons (45 milliliters) milk

2 tablespoons (30 milliliters) whipping cream

Place the bass fillets in an oval dish. Add the wine, half of the shallots, and the tarragon. Marinate for two hours. Keep the marinade.

Dice half of the fish and place in a food processor. Add salt and pepper and egg whites and blend for two minutes. Add the 3/4 cup (180 milliliters) milk and blend for another 3 minutes.

Cook the asparagus in salted water, then trim off the stringy parts.

Dice the remaining fish. Butter the inside of 4 soufflé dishes (4 inches or 10 centimeters in diameter) and fill them half full with the fish mixture. Add the diced fish and 3 asparagus to each mold. Fill the rest of the soufflé molds with fish mixture, cover with aluminum foil, and bake in a pan of hot water in a preheated 425° oven for 15 minutes.

In a saucepan, heat the oil and add the remaining shallots and the mushrooms. Cook slowly for 4 minutes. Add the reserved marinade. Simmer to evaporate. Add the clam juice and milk. Cover and simmer the sauce for 15 minutes, then add cream and blend in the food processor.

Unmold the pâtés and pour the sauce over before serving.

Serves: 4

Mon Ami Restaurant

Proprietors:
June Berridge and Wanda Hames
Chef: Guy Lafontaine

731 South Highway 101
Mercado del Sol
Solana Beach, California 92075
(714) 755-6955

Four years ago, the question was: Can a former teacher and a retired nurse successfully translate a long-standing culinary desire into one of southern California's premier French restaurants? The answer today is an emphatic Yes! June Berridge and Wanda Hames's **Mon Ami Restaurant**, located in the sleepy sea community of Solana Beach about 15 miles north of downtown San Diego, is now one of the finest French dining establishments on the West Coast.

Upon entering the restaurant, you will be greeted by simple elegance: a warm homey atmosphere punctuated by dark woods, candlelight, attractively arranged bottles of wine in cabinets, and either soft classical or jazz music. Your entrée, which is served with soup, salad, fresh vegetables, and potato, can be chosen from the regular menu (perhaps

Le Canard au Grand Marnier or Les Tournedos aux Trois Sauces) or from the daily specialty menu that always includes veal and seafood entrées and sometimes exotic items such as Fresh Rabbit of the Black Forest — all expertly prepared by the sensational young chef du cuisine, Guy Lafontaine. One of the youngest chefs in the industry — only 22 years old — this French Canadian began his restaurant career at age 14 and became a head chef at age 17. Chef Lafontaine is equally as skilled as a pastry chef, so when you plan your meal at Mon Ami, be sure to leave room for dessert.

Mon Ami Restaurant is open seven days a week for dinner. Dress is casual, reservations are suggested, and all major credit cards are accepted. Prices are moderately expensive.

FEUILLES D'ÉPINARDS LAFONTAINE

6 slices bacon, finely sliced

1/2 pound (227 grams) fresh mushrooms, sliced

1 tablespoon (15 milliliters) red wine vinegar

3 tablespoons (45 milliliters) olive oil

juice of 1 fresh lemon

dash of Tabasco sauce

1 tablespoon (15 milliliters) Worcestershire sauce

salt and freshly ground pepper, to taste

2 bunches fresh spinach leaves

1 ounce (30 milliliters) brandy

3 red tomatoes, sliced in 4 slices each

Cook the bacon in a large sauté pan until crisp. Add the mushrooms and mix together. Remove from heat and add vinegar, oil, lemon juice, Tabasco, and Worcestershire sauce. Then add the salt, pepper, and spinach leaves. Flame with brandy. Mix quickly and serve immediately on the slices of tomato.

Serves: 4

Wine: *White Burgundy (French) or a California Chardonnay*

Irmgard and Heinz Gerstle, the owners of the **Normandy French Restaurant** on Madison Street, have devoted themselves for over 20 years to maintaining a standard of excellence in cuisine, ambiance, and service. Mr. Gerstle is also the chef, having received extensive training in Europe. They are perpetually trying new recipes and keep an eye open for artifacts and special features which might add to their restaurant's cozy European feeling.

The Trances de Celeri Rave Vinaigrette is an example of the Normandy's originality. The Escalope de Veau "Marie Antoinette" sautéed in butter, served in casserole with mushroom sauce, and topped with cheese, and Le Coq au Beaujolai "Paul Blanc" are the chef's specialties. The Normandy has one of the country's largest selection of Burgundy wines. All price ranges are available. A natural, delicious dessert is framboises Foret Noir.

The Normandy French Restaurant is open for lunch Tuesday through Saturday 11:30 a.m.–2:30 p.m., for dinner Tuesday through Sunday 5:00 p.m.–10:30 p.m. It is closed on Mondays and during the first two weeks of July. Jackets and ties are suggested wear for gentlemen, and all major credit cards are honored. Prices are moderately expensive.

Normandy French Restaurant

1515 Madison Street
Denver, Colorado 80206
(303) 321-3311

Proprietor/Chef: Heinz E. Gerstle

ESCARGOTS BOURGUIGNONNE

4 dozen snails

4 dozen snail shells

4 pounds (1.8 kilograms) soft butter

1 bunch parsley

1 medium-sized yellow onion, peeled

10 cloves garlic, peeled

10 shallots, peeled

2 ounces (56 grams) salt

2 ounces (56 grams) ground white pepper

2 ounces (60 milliliters) Worcestershire sauce

2 ounces (56 grams) Maggi seasoning

2 ounces (56 grams) Coleman's dry mustard

3 drops Tabasco sauce

Drain the snails, wash in cold water, and let drain again. Set aside. Whip the butter in a mixer.

To prepare snail butter: mince the parsley, onion, garlic, and shallots through the fine blade of a meat grinder. Then add the remaining ingredients and mix well. Add this mixed seasoned vegetable mixture to the whipped butter and mix well. Correct the seasoning if necessary.

Put some of the snail butter into the empty shells first, then stuff the snails into the shells and top them with a generous serving of the snail butter. Place the stuffed shells onto escargot plates and heat in a very hot oven until they brown and sizzle well. Serve hot.

Serves: 6-8

Wine: *Macon Villages, Blanc*

Pierre's Quorum Restaurant

Proprietor: Pierre Wolfe

Colfax at Grant
Denver, Colorado 80203
(303) 861-8686

Pierre's Quorum Restaurant, located directly opposite the State Capitol Building, is a lovely and prestigious place in which to dine. Proprietor Pierre Wolfe is a popular local personality, appearing frequently on radio and television programs to explain or prepare his original cuisine. A native of Alsace-Lorraine, he received his chef's training at the Hotel and Restaurant Management School in Switzerland. He worked in Lucerne and Lausanne before moving to Denver in 1950.

Tapestries and original art adorn the walls at Pierre's Quorum. There are candles and fresh flowers set at your table, and light classical music plays in the background.

Veal Ritz Carlton, a scallopini with diced sweetbreads in chanterelle mushroom sauce with avocado garnish, is the house specialty. Another favorite is Medallions of Beef Tenderloin Marengo, prime beef crested with crab meat, mushrooms, and a light brandy sauce.

There is an extensive, reasonably priced wine list of imported and domestic vintages. For a delicious dessert, try the Almond Crepes topped with raspberry sauce or Oranges Morocco.

Pierre's Quorum Restaurant is open for lunch and dinner Monday through Friday, and for dinner only on Saturday. Jackets are required, as are reservations, preferably made one or two days in advance. All major credit cards are honored. Prices are moderately expensive.

CHEF PIERRE'S ORANGES MOROCCO

2 tablespoons (30 milliliters) butter

2 tablespoons (30 milliliters) granulated sugar

2 tablespoons (30 milliliters) brown sugar

6 oranges, peeled and thinly sliced

2 tablespoons (30 milliliters) finely chopped almonds

1/2 cup (120 milliliters) finely chopped dates

1/4 cup (60 milliliters) brandy

6-8 scoops ice cream or orange sherbet

Heat the butter in a chafing dish. Add the granulated and brown sugars and allow to caramelize, being careful not to burn the sugar. Place the orange slices in the sugar-butter mixture and cook for 2-3 minutes. Add the almonds and dates and heat thoroughly. Pour the brandy over and ignite to flame. When the fire has gone out, spoon the mixture over the ice cream or sherbet and serve.

Serves: 6-8

Mon Petit French Restaurant

Proprietor/Chef: Frank Pourdad

7000 West 38th Avenue
Wheat Ridge, Colorado
(303) 424-4700

Mon Petit is a charming classic French restaurant established six years ago by owner/chef Frank Pourdad, who converted an authentic 19th century residence into an elegant dining environment that is lavishly appointed with oil paintings, chandeliers, wood paneling, warm floor and window coverings, and green plants. The freshly cut flowers that are placed on each table daily add to the overall feeling that you are dining in a fine home.

The menu at Mon Petit is equally lavish, yet there is nothing appearing that is compromised — no obligatory listings to fill the page. Each offering is afforded the same care in preparation as another because each item is a specialty. Mr. Pourdad, whose prior experience has been as as restaurant manager and caterer, first offers the diner a choice of hot or cold hors d'oeuvres, including excellent pâté de foie gras de Strasbourg and a special Crepe de Crabe au Mon Petit. After onion soup gratinée or vichyssoise, you may want to try a traditional French entrée, such as a superb Filet of Sole Véronique or Steak au Poivre, or perhaps one of the more unique menu items, such as the Alaskan King Crab de Jonghe, Bottom in Sherry, or the Chicken Médaillons Piccata. Salade Cesar for two is a good choice to follow. The dessert list is especially kind to those of us suffering from chocolate cravings. All in all, dining at Mon Petit is a rewarding experience for the discerning gourmet and, especially, for those of us who long to be.

Mon Petit is open for lunch and dinner, Tuesday through Saturday. Seating is limited, therefore, reservations are required. Jackets are prescribed, major credit cards are honored. Prices are moderately expensive.

Restaurant

Kahala Hilton Hotel
5000 Kahala Avenue
Honolulu, Hawaii 96816
(808) 734-2211

ROAST DUCKLING WAIALAE

2 4-pound (1.8-kilogram) ducklings

salt and pepper, to taste

1/4 cup (60 milliliters) sugar

1/2 cup (120 milliliters) wine vinegar

2 oranges

3/4 cup (180 milliliters) red wine

2 cups (480 milliliters) heated Espagnole Sauce (brown sauce), not too thick

1 cup (240 milliliters) water or wine

Tabasco sauce, to taste

Kitchen Bouquet (optional)

16 pieces lychee

12 pieces tangerine

16 slices banana

1 ounce (30 milliliters) Grand Marnier

1 ounce (30 milliliters) brandy

Rub ducklings with salt and pepper. Roast at 350-375° for 1-1 1/2 hours or until tender.

Caramelize the sugar in a saucepan. Add vinegar and simmer for a few minutes.

Peel the oranges with a julienne scraper. In a separate pan, boil the orange peel julienne in red wine for 5 minutes. Squeeze orange juice into the caramel sauce. Add heated Espagnole Sauce and simmer for 15 minutes.

When the ducklings are done, remove them from the roasting pan and discard the fat. Deglaze the pan with the water or wine and add this stock to the sauce. Simmer a little longer. Strain the sauce, then add the orange peel and wine mixture. Add a few drops of Tabasco to taste. (If the sauce is not dark enough, add a little Kitchen Bouquet for color.)

Carve each duckling into 4 pieces and arrange in a flat skillet. Sprinkle with lychee, tangerine, and banana slices. Heat over a burner. Flame with Grand Marnier and brandy. Pour the sauce over the ducklings. Suggestion: serve with buttered wild rice and spiced peaches.

Serves: 4

Michel's at the Colony Surf is a part of the luxury resort complex known as the Colony Surf Hotel, and is situated above Honolulu with a spectacular view of the curve at Waikiki and Diamond Head. The scene is accented by the decor of Michel's—crystal chandeliers, silver table service, walnut wall panels. The combined effect is elegant and romantic and would complement any dining experience. But this restaurant does not rely solely on its location and decor—it also serves fine food.

J. Hans Strasser, the executive vice-president and general manager, is a native of Austria and has enjoyed more than 20 years in the restaurant and hotel business. In 1970, he arrived in Hawaii to direct the operations of the hotel and to open the new restaurant. His success with Michel's, in particular, is evidenced by the many awards the restaurant has received since its opening.

The success of Michel's must also be credited to its kitchen staff now headed by 25-year-old executive chef Gordon Hopkins, a native of the Islands. Despite his relative youth, Chef Hopkins has directly benefited from the experiences of some of America's great master chefs during tenures at several major American restaurants. In addition to the many familiar French dishes served, one can also enjoy the special creations by Chef Hopkins, including the house specialty, Longe de Veau, Roti (roast loin of veal with a light cognac creme sauce). The menu is further enhanced by local fish delicacies. An extensive wine list is also available.

Michel's at the Colony Surf is open daily for breakfast, lunch (except Saturday), and dinner. Reservations are suggested, jackets for men are required after 6 p.m., and all major credit cards are accepted. Prices are expensive.

Michel's at the Colony Surf

2895 Kalakaua Avenue
Honolulu, Hawaii 96815
(808) 923-6552

Chef: Gordon W.K. Hopkins

ROAST LOIN OF VEAL

2 ounces (56 grams) flour

2 pounds (980 grams) strip loin of veal, well trimmed, no fat

2 ounces (56 grams) butter

salt and pepper, to taste

3 sprigs fresh thyme

4 ounces (120 milliliters) veal stock or beef consommé

2 ounces (60 milliliters) cognac, Courvoisier preferred

6 ounces (180 milliliters) demi-glaze (brown gravy, preferably made from veal bones)

2 ounces (60 milliliters) heavy cream

pinch of cayenne pepper

pinch of fresh parsley

Lightly flour the veal loin. Heat the butter in a pan and lightly brown the veal on both sides. Season with salt, pepper, and thyme. In the same pan, bake the veal in a preheated 350° oven for 10 minutes. The veal should be medium. Remove the veal from the pan and set aside.

To prepare Cognac Creme Sauce: remove the fat from the pan and heat the pan so it is very hot without burning the drippings. Add the veal stock, Courvoisier, and demi-glaze. Let the sauce reduce at a low temperature until slightly thickened. Add the cream, salt and pepper, cayenne pepper, and parsley. Bring to a boil, then simmer until it reaches the desired consistency.

To serve: place the veal on a silver tray garnished with colorful, attractive vegetables. Slice the veal loin on the bias very thinly. Ladle sauce onto a dinner plate, then place veal slices on the plate on top of the sauce.

Serves: 4

Wine: *Fumé Blanc, Robert Mondavi*

Salishan Lodge

Chef: Franz J. Buck

Gleneden Beach, Oregon 97388
(503) 764-2371

The **Gourmet Dining Room of the Salishan Lodge** presents its international cuisine in a quiet, informal setting. The restaurant draws its recipes essentially from French and American sources, but will, from time to time, present ethnic specialties from all over the world.

One of the most requested of their cold appetizers is the Gallatine of Duckling (a slice of pâté in a duck casing with Cumberland sauce). Other delicacies are Oysters On The Half Shell fresh from Oregon's Tillamook Bay, and Smoked Salmon Canapes with slices of sweet onions and capers.

Their hot hors d'oeuvres selections include the unusual Crepes Au Roquefort, Metaxa (thin pancakes with a Roquefort cheese cream filling flavored with Metaxa Greek brandy) and Koniginpastete ("The Queen's Pastry"—a patty shell filled with sweetbreads, mushrooms, veal, and a special cream sauce).

Executive Chef Franz Buck has come up with several very special original entrées that include Carpet Bagger Steak (filet mignon stuffed with Pacific oysters), Broiled Lemon Chicken with Fine Herbs, and Médaillons of Veal Noilly Prat. The seafood entrées are also special.

Available on two days' notice, for four to eight persons, are Coulibiac (a fillet of Chinook salmon layered with mushrooms, rice, onions, shrimp, all baked in a crust and served with Hollandaise Sauce) and Vinison Baden-Baden (leg of aged New Zealand deer, browned and braised in its own juices and served with currant jelly, Berny almond potatoes, pear half, and sour cream sauce).

The Gourmet Dining Room is open every day for dinner only. Reservations are not required. Gentlemen must wear jackets. All major credit cards are accepted. Prices are moderate to moderately expensive.

MÉDAILLONS OF VEAL NOILLY PRAT

6 poached artichoke bottoms

salt and lemon juice, to taste

3-4 ounces (90-120 milliliters) Herb Boursin cheese

4 4-ounce (112-gram) veal scallopines

white pepper, to taste

clarified butter, to sauté

vermouth, to deglaze, Noilly Prat preferred

MSG, to taste

lemon wedges, parsley sprig, and 1 whole crayfish poached in salted water, to garnish

Purée the artichoke bottoms, salt, lemon juice, and cheese in a blender. Reserve.

Heat a sauté pan. Season the veal lightly with salt and white pepper, then fry in clarified butter for about 15 seconds per side. Transfer to a warmed serving platter.

Pour off the excess butter, then deglaze the pan with vermouth. Reduce to 1/8 the original volume, then add the artichoke purée (2-3 ounces or 60-90 milliliters per person) to thicken the sauce. Bring close to boiling and adjust the seasoning with salt, white pepper, and MSG.

Ladle the finished sauce over the veal, garnish with lemon wedges, parsley, and crayfish, and serve.

Serves: 2

The **Pettygrove House Restaurant** takes a unique approach to what might be called "*Nouvelle Cuisine* American-style" — they use the freshest ingredients, prepare light sauces and adapt classic recipes into new preparations which display a strong American and regional influence.

There are three small attractive dining rooms on the parlor floor of this Victorian home. The setting is informal, intimate, and candlelit. Recorded classical music plays in the background.

A small wine list emphasizes the products of California, Oregon, and Washington, with just a few French vintages.

Appetizers include Escargots in Tartelet with bacon, mushrooms, and leeks in red wine sauce; and a Jewish-style chicken liver pâté with onions, paprika, and hard-boiled eggs.

The Pettygrove House prepares a savory Pacific Bouillabaisse (several varieties of seafood all simmered in a broth of fish stock, white wine, garlic, onions, leeks, fennel, tomatoes, and saffron). Their Rolled Stuffed Breast of Veal is delicious fancy Oregon veal stuffed with Italian sausage, fresh herbs, and spinach, braised in a savory brown veal stock with white wine and tomatoes added. The menu announces that "seasonal specialties are available at the mercy of the oceans, streams, fields and forests."

The Pettygrove House serves lunch Tuesday through Friday, and dinner Tuesday through Saturday. Call ahead for reservations. You are free to dress in a casual, comfortable manner. American Express, Visa, and Mastercharge are accepted. Prices are moderate to moderately expensive.

Pettygrove House Restaurant

2287 N.W. Pettygrove
Portland, Oregon
(503) 223-6025   Chef: Fred Finger

BREAST OF CHICKEN WITH CRAB SAUCE

4 tablespoons (60 milliliters) soft butter

4-6 10-ounce (280-gram) chicken breasts, skinned and boned

juice of 1/2 lemon

salt and pepper, to taste

meat from 1 fresh 2-2 1/2-pound (.9-1.1-kilogram) Dungeness crab

1 ounce (30 milliliters) cognac

1 generous cup (250 milliliters) crab sauce, prepared

1 scant cup (230 milliliters) Mousseline sauce, prepared

carrots, celery, and leek, julienne, to garnish

Brush 1/2 the butter with a pastry brush on the inside of a 9-inch (23-centimeter) skillet that is *not* cast iron. Arrange the breasts in the pan and brush with the remaining butter. Sprinkle the lemon juice over the chicken and season lightly with salt and pepper. Cover with a buttered round of waxed paper and the lid. Bake in a 425° oven for 20 minutes or until tender. Remove chicken to a warmer and drain, then cover loosely while preparing the sauce and garnish.

Pour off most of the fat in the skillet and reduce the pan juices to a demi-glaze. Add the crabmeat to the pan and toss to coat with juices. Add cognac, but do not flame. Reduce for 1 minute, then add crab sauce and Mousseline sauce, swirling them together until combined and heated through. *Do not boil!*

Prepare the garnish by blanching the carrots, celery, and leek separately, then steaming together with butter.

Place the breasts in the center of each of 4 plates. Spoon equal amounts of sauce around each of them, distributing the crab attractively on the plates. Garnish with little bundles of cooked julienne carrots, celery, and leek.

Serves: 4-6

Wine: *Chardonnay or dry Sauvignon blanc*

Directory of Fine Dining

ALABAMA
Mobile (Area Code 205)
Constantine's
1500 Government Street
471-3375

ALASKA
Anchorage (907)
House of Lords Restaurant
The Sheffield House
720 West Fifth Avenue
276-5404

ARIZONA
Phoenix (602)
The Golden Eagle
201 North Central
257-7700
Continental

Scottsdale (602)
La Champagne
7171 North Scottsdale Road
991-3800

La Chaumiere
6910 Main Street
946-5115

ARKANSAS
Little Rock (501)
Anderson's Cajun's Wharf
2400 Cantrell Road
375-5351

Leather Bottle
1505 Revsanen Park Road
664-6444

CALIFORNIA
Beverly Hills (213)
Le Bella Fontana
Beverly Wilshire Hotel
9500 Wilshire Boulevard
275-4282
French

The Bistro Garden
176 North Canon Drive
550-3900

L'Escoffier
Beverly Hilton Hotel
9876 Wilshire Boulevard
274-7777
French

La Famiglia
453 North Canon Drive
276-6208
Italian

Mandarin
430 Camden Drive
272-0267
Chinese

Burlingame (415)
Kee Joon's
433 Airport Boulevard
348-1122
Chinese

Carmel (408)
Casanova
Fifth between San Carlos
and Mission
625-0501
Italian/French

L'Escargot
Mission Street near 4th
624-4914
French

Hog's Breath Inn
San Carlos between 5th & 6th
625-1044
American

Marquis
San Carlos & 4th Street
624-8068
French

Patisserie Boissiere
Mission between Ocean & 7th
624-5008
French

Rafaello
Mission between Ocean & 7th
524-1541
Italian

Shabu-Shabu
Carmel Plaza
Mission between Ocean & 7th
625-2828
Japanese

El Topo
San Carlos between 5th & 6th
624-7388
Mexican

Los Angeles (213)
Bernard's
The Biltmore
515 South Olive
624-0183
French

Chasen's
9039 Beverly Boulevard
271-2168

Chung King
11538 Pico Boulevard
477-4917
Chinese

Le Dome
8720 Sunset Boulevard
659-6919
French

Emilio's Ristorante
6602 Melrose Avenue
935-4922
Italian

L'Ermitage
730 North La Cienega Boulevard
652-5840
French

Francois
Arco Plaza
555 South Flower Street
680-2727
French

Ma Maison
8368 Melrose Avenue
655-1991
French

L'Orangerie
903 North La Cienega
652-9770
French

Perino's
4101 Wilshire Boulevard
383-1221
French

Ristorante Chianti
7383 Melrose Avenue
653-8333
Italian

Scandia
9040 Sunset Boulevard
272-9521

Le St. Germain
5955 Melrose Avenue
467-1108
French

Tepparod
4649 Melbourne Avenue
666-9919
Thai

A Thousand Cranes
New Otani Hotel
120 South Los Angeles Street
629-1200

The Windsor
3198 West Seventh Street
382-1261
French

Yamato
2025 Avenue of the Stars
277-1840
Japanese

San Diego (714)
Anthony's Star of the Sea Room
Harbor Drive and Ash
232-7408
Seafood

La Chaumine
1466 Garnet Street
272-8540
French

Fontainbleau Room
Little America Westgate Hotel
1055 Second Avenue
238-1818
French

Lubach's
2101 North Harbor Drive
232-5129
French

La Maison des Pescadoux
2265 Bacon Street at
West Point Loma Boulevard
225-9579
Seafood

Nino's
4501 Mission Bay Drive
274-3141
Italian

Thee Bungalow
4996 West Point Loma
Boulevard at Bacon
224-2884
American

San Francisco (415)
Agadir
746 Broadway
397-6305
Moroccan

Alexis Restaurant
1001 California Street
885-6400
French

Amelio's
1630 Powell Street
397-4339
Continental

Le Beaujolais
2415 Clement Street
752-3921
French

Blue Boar Inn
1713 Lombard Street
567-8424

Carnelian Room
Bank of America Center
555 California Street
433-7500
French

Le Central
453 Bush Street
391-2233
French

Chez Panisse
1517 Shattuck Avenue
548-5525
French

Le Club
1250 Jones Street
771-5400
French

Empress of China
China Trade Center
838 Grant Avenue
434-1345
Chinese

Ernie's Restaurant
847 Montgomery Street
397-5969
French

L'Etoile
1075 California Street
771-1529
French

Fleur de Lys
777 Sutter Street
673-7779
French

Four Seasons French Room
The Clift Hotel
Geary at Taylor
775-4700
French

Garden Court
Sheraton-Palace Hotel
Market and New
Montgomery Streets
392-8600
American

Gaylord India Restaurant
900 North Point
Ghirardelli Square
771-8822
Indian

Hunan Restaurant
924 Sansome Street
956-7727
Chinese

Imperial Palace
919 Grant Avenue
982-4440
Chinese

India House
350 Jackson Street
392-0744
Indian

Jack's Restaurant
615 Sacramento Street
986-9854

Kan's
708 Grant Avenue
982-2388
Chinese

Mama's
1177 California Street
928-1004
American

The Mandarin
900 North Point
673-8812
Chinese

La Mirabelle
1326 Powell Street
421-3374
French

North Beach Restaurant
1512 Stockton Street
392-1700
Italian

L'Orangerie
419 Farrell Street
776-3600
French

Restaurant Orsi
375 Bush Street
981-6535

Paprikas Fono
Ghirardelli Square
441-1223
Hungarian

Rene Verdon's Le Trianon
242 O'Farrell Street
982-9353
French

Le Rhone
3614 Balboa Street
387-4559
French

Shandygaff Cafe Restaurant
1760 Polk Street
441-1760
Vegetarian

Szechwan
2209 Polk Street
474-8282
Chinese

Tadich Grill
240 California Street
391-2373
Seafood

Trader Vic's
20 Cosmo Place
776-2232
Chinese/Polynesian

Sausalito (415)

Le Vivoir
Casa Madrone Hotel
156 Bulkley Avenue
332-1850
French

COLORADO
Boulder (303)

Red Lion Inn
Boulder Canyon Road
442-9368
Continental

Denver (303)

The Athenian
5501 East Colfax Avenue
377-8478
Greek

Bavarian Inn
490 South Colorado Boulevard
377-0208
German

Benardi & Sons
2631 Broadway
449-9460
Italian

The Buckhorn Exchange
1000 Osage Street
534-9505
Steak House

Cafe Promenade
1430 Larimer Street
893-2692
Continental

Downtown Broker
17th and Champa Streets
893-5065
American

Dudley's
1120 East 6th Avenue
744-8634
French

Emerson Street East
900 Colfax Avenue
832-1349
American

La Fontanella
1700 East Evans Avenue
778-8598
Italian

Golden Dragon
1467 Nelson Street
237-4144
Chinese

Mataam Fez
4609 East Colfax Avenue
355-7037
Moroccan

San Marco Room
Brown Palace Hotel
17th Street and Tremont Place
825-3111
American

Tante Louise
4900 East Colfax Avenue
355-4488
French

R. Valentino's
1469 Pearl Street
722-1604
Vegetarian

CONNECTICUT
Greenwich (203)

Cinquante-Cinq
55 Arch Street
869-5641
French

Ridgefield (203)

The Inn at Ridgefield
20 West Lane/Route 35
438-8282

DELAWARE
Wilmington (302)

Columbus Inn
2216 Pennsylvania Avenue
571-1492
Continental

DISTRICT OF COLUMBIA (202)

Germaine's
2400 Wisconsin Avenue
965-1185
Asian

Jean Pierre
1835 K Street N.W.
466-2022
French

Le Lion d'Or
1150 Connecticut Avenue N.W.
296-7972
French

Le Pavillon
1820 K Street N.W.
833-3846
French

Le Provencal
1234 20th Street N.W.
223-2420
French

El Tio Pepe
2809 M Street N.W.
337-0730
Spanish

FLORIDA
Coral Gables (305)

Le Festival
2120 Salzedo Street
442-8545
French

Wiffenpoof
2728-32 Ponce de Leon
Boulevard
445-6603
Continental

Hialeah (305)

El Segundo Viajante
2846 Palm Avenue
888-5465
Latin

Miami (305)

Cafe Chauveron
9561 East Bay Harbor Drive
866-8779
French

The Depot
5830 South Dixie Highway
665-6261
American

Food Among the Flowers
21 N.E. 36th Street
576-0000

Prince Hamlet
8301 Biscayne Boulevard
754-4400
Scandinavian

Raimondo
201 N.W. 79th Street
757-9403
Continental

Tiger Teahouse
2235 Biscayne Boulevard
573-2689
Chinese

Wong's
12420 Biscayne Boulevard
891-4313
Chinese

Miami Beach (305)

The Forge
432 Arthur Godfrey Road
538-8533
American

GEORGIA
Atlanta (404)

Bernard's
1193 Collier Road N.W.
352-2778
French

Nicolai's Roof
Atlanta Hilton
255 Courtland Street N.W.
659-2000
French

Smyrna (305)

Aunt Fanny's Cabin
375 Campbell Road
436-9026
Southern

HAWAII
Honolulu (808)

L'Auberge
117 Hekili Street
Kailua
262-4835

Bagwell's 2424
Hyatt Regency
2424 Kalakaua Avenue
922-9292
Continental

Barrio Fiesta
1887-A Kalakaua Avenue
941-9794
Filipino

Le Cafe de Paris
1778 Ala Moana Bolveard
at Discovery Bay
947-6467
French

Canlis'
2100 Kalakaua Avenue
923-2324

Champeaux's
1777 Ala Moana Boulevard
949-3811

Chez Michel
2126-B Kalakaua Avenue
923-0626
French

Dickens British Pub
1221 Kapiolani Boulevard
531-2727
British

Helena's Hawaiian Foods
1364 North King Street
845-8044
Hawaiian

Mekong
1295 Beretaine Street
521-2025
Thai

Nick's Fishmarket
Waikiki Gateway Hotel
2070 Kalakaua Avenue
955-6333

Rex's Ristorante
2310 Kuhio Avenue
923-7618
Continental

The Third Floor
Hawaiian Regent Hotel
2552 Kalakaua Avenue
922-6611

Winter Garden
Kahala Mall
Waialae at Kilauea
732-5505
Chinese

IDAHO
Boise (208)

The Gamekeeper
Ow Yhee Plaza Hotel
1109 Main Street
344-7631
Continental

ILLINOIS
Chicago (312)

Ann Sathers
925 West Belmont
348-2378
Swedish

The Bakery
2218 North Lincoln Avenue
472-6942
Continental

Cafe de Paris
1260 North Dearborn Parkway
943-6080
French

Doro's
871 North Rush Street
266-1414
Italian

L'Escargot
2925 North Halsted Street
525-5525
French

La Fontaine
2440 North Clark
525-1800
French

La Fontanella
2414 South Oakley
927-5249
Italian

Gateway to India
1543 North Wells
642-7755
Indian

Golden Ox
1580 North Clyborn
664-0781
German

Greek Islands
766 West Jackson
782-9855
Greek

Heartland Cafe
7000 North Glenwood
465-8005
Vegetarian

Jovan
16 East Huron Street
944-7766
French

Manny's
1139 South Jefferson
939-2855
Jewish

Morton's
1050 State Street
266-4820
American

Nick's Fish Market
1 First National Plaza
621-1200
Seafood

Le Perroquet
70 East Walton
944-7990
French

Dr. Shen's
1050 North State Street
440-2322
Chinese

Tango
3170 North Sheridan
935-0350
Seafood

Thai Villa
3811 North Lincoln
472-9478
Thai

INDIANA

Camby (317)

Chez Jean Restaurant Francais
Indiana 67
831-0870

Indianapolis (317)

Chanteclair sur le Toit
Holiday Inn Airport
2501 South High School Road
244-7378
French

King Cole
7 North Meridian Street
638-5588
Continental

New Orleans House
8845 Township Line Road
298-9670
Seafood

IOWA

Amana (319)

Ox Yoke Inn
Main Street
622-3441

Pella (515)

Strawtown Inn
1111 Washington Street
628-4043

KANSAS

Kansas City (816)

Cousin John's
Ramada Inn
Overland Park
8787 Reeder
888-8440

KENTUCKY

Louisville (502)

La Cuisiniere
1285 Bardstown Road
456-6815
French

Old Stone Inn
Simpsonville via U.S. 60
or I-64
722-8882

LOUISIANA

New Orleans (504)

Antoine's
713 St. Louis
581-4422
French

Begue's
Royal Sonesta Hotel
300 Bourbon Street
586-0300

Caribbean Room
Pontchartrain Hotel
2031 St. Charles Avenue
524-0581

Christian's
3835 Iberville Street
482-4924
French

Crozier's Restaurant Francais
9301 Lake Forest Boulevard
241-8220
French

Delmonico
1300 St. Charles Avenue
525-4937
Creole

Dragon's Garden
3100 17th Metairie
834-9065
Chinese

Jonathan
714 North Rampart
586-1930
Continental

Louis XVI
829 Toulouse Street
581-7000
French

Masson's Restaurant Francais
7200 Ponchartrain Boulevard
283-2525
French

Pascal's Manale
1838 Napoleon Avenue
895-4877
Italian

Sazerac
Fairmont Hotel
University Place
529-7111
Continental

MAINE

Hancock (207)

Le Domaine
U.S. Route 1
422-3395
French

Portland (207)

Boone's Restaurant
6 Custom House Wharf
774-5725

MARYLAND

Baltimore (301)

Cafe des Artistes
9 Hopkins Plaza
837-6600
French

Faidley's
Lexington Market
Eutaw and Lexington Streets
727-4898
Maryland Oysters

Haussner's
3244 Eastern Avenue
327-8365
German

Marconi's
106 West Saratoga Street
752-9286
Continental

Pimlico Hotel
5301 Park Heights Avenue
664-8014
American

Prime Rib
Horizon House Apartments
1101 North Calvert Street
539-1804
Steak House

Sacha's
80 North Charles Avenue
752-5228
Crepes

Tio Pepe
10 East Franklin Street
539-4675
Continental/Spanish

Cockeysville (301)

The Milton Inn
York Road at Sparks
771-4366
French and Italian

Columbia (301)

The King's Contrivance
Route 32 at Route 29
995-0500
Continental

MASSACHUSETTS

Boston (617)

Anthony's Pier 4
140 Northern Avenue
423-6363
Seafood

Cafe Budapest
90 Exeter Street
Copley Square
734-3388
Hungarian

Durgin Park
30 North Market Street
227-2038
American

Francesca's and Villa Francesca
147 and 150 Richmond Street
523-8826
Italian

The Ritz Dining Room
Ritz-Carlton Hotel
15 Arlington Street
536-5700
French

Cambridge (617)

The Rendezvous
24 Holyoke Street
547-5005
Vietnamese, French

The Voyagers
45 1/2 Mount Auburn Street
354-1718
Nouvelle Cuisine

Newton Centre (617)

The Modern Gourmet
81R Union Street
969-1320
Nouvelle Cuisine

MICHIGAN

Dearborn (313)

Dearborn Inn
20301 Oakwood Boulevard
271-2700
Country

Detroit (313)

Aldo's
1914 Kelly
839-2180
Italian

Aliette's
Porter at 24th
554-0902
French

Al's Lounge
West End at South
841-5677
Hungarian

Benno's
8027 Agnes
499-0040
Continental

Brau Haus
1977 East Woodbridge
259-1212
German

Cardinali's
3485 Mitchell
267-9622
Italian

The Caucus Club
150 West Congress Street
965-4970

Chung's
3177 Cass Avenue
831-1100
Chinese

The Money Tree
333 West Fort Street
961-2445
Continental

New Hellas
583 Monroe
961-5544
Greek

The Pontchartrain French Wine Cellars
234 West Larned
963-1785

The Sheik
316 East Lafayette
964-8441
Arabic

Grosse Pointe Park (313)

Harvest Park
15406 Mack
343-0679
Vegetarian

MINNESOTA
Minneapolis (612)

Le Carrousel
Radisson Hotel
Wabasha at Kellogg Boulevard
222-7711
Continental

The 510 Haute Cuisine
510 Groveland Avenue
874-6440
Continental

Flame Room
Radisson Hotel
333-2181
Continental

Forepaugh's
276 South Exchange Street
224-5606
American

Horatio Hornblower's
345 Wabasha Street
227-8781
Seafood

International Rosewood Room
Northstar Inn
618 Second Avenue South
338-2288
French

The Little Prince
1403 Harmon Place
338-0900
Continental

Murray's
26 South Sixth Street
339-0909
Steaks

New French Cafe
128 North Fourth Street
338-3790
French

Orion Room
50th Floor, IDS Tower
372-3772
Continental

MISSISSIPPI
Vicksburg (601)

Old Southern Tea Room
1313 Walnut Street
636-3433

MISSOURI
Chesterfield (314)

L'Auberge Bretonne
13419 Chesterfield Shopping Plaza
Olive Street Road at Woods Mill
878-7706
French

Kansas City (816)

Alameda Roof
Alameda Hotel
Wornall Road at Ward Parkway
756-1500

Arthur Bryant's Barbecue
1727 Brooklyn
231-1123
Barbecue

La Bonne Bouchee
618 Ward Parkway
931-5230
French

Gojo's
4193 Broadway
561-2501
Japanese

Houlchan's Old Place
4743 Pennsylvania
561-3141
American

Le Mediterranee
4742 Pennsylvania
561-3016
French

The Olive Tree
4916 Main
753-1332
Moroccan

Plaza III
4749 Pennsylvania
753-0000

The Prospect
4109 Pennsylvania
753-2277
American

The Savoy
9th and Central
842-3890
Seafood

Tony's
423 Southwest Boulevard
471-9833
Seafood

St. Louis (314)

Anthony's
Equitable Building
10 South Broadway
231-2434
Continental

Dominic's
5101 Wilson Avenue
771-1632
Continental

Giovanni's
5201 Shaw Avenue
772-5958
Italian

Henry VIII Inn and Lodge
4690 North Lindbergh
731-4888

Jefferson Avenue Boarding House
3265 South Jefferson Avenue
771-4100
American

Tenderloin Room
Chase-Park Plaza Hotel
212 North King's Highway
361-2500
Steaks

Tony's
826 North Broadway
231-7007

MONTANA
Billings (406)

Golden Belle Dining Room
Northern Hotel
Broadway and 1st Avenue North
245-5121

NEBRASKA
Omaha (402)

Le Cafe de Paris
1228 South 6th Street
344-0227

NEVADA
Las Vegas (702)

Alpine Village Inn
3003 Paradise Road
734-6888
German

Golden Steer
308 West Sahara Avenue
384-4470
American

Palace Court
Caesar's Palace Hotel
3570 Las Vegas Boulevard South
731-7100

Phillips Supperhouse
4545 West Sahara Avenue
873-5222
American

Regency Room
Sands Hotel
3355 Las Vegas Boulevard South
733-5000
Continental

NEW HAMPSHIRE
New London (603)

Hide-Away Lodge
Twin Lakes Villa Road
526-4861

NEW JERSEY
West Orange (201)

The Manor
111 Prospect Avenue
731-2360

NEW MEXICO
Sante Fe (505)

The Compound
653 Canyon Road
982-4353
French

NEW YORK
Buffalo (716)

Mastrantonio's
899 Niagara Falls Boulevard
836-3366
Continental

The Park Lane Manor House
Gates Circle
885-3250
British

Pepie's Plum
102 La Salle Arterial
285-2000

Plaza Suite
1 M & T Plaza
842-5555

Polonia
193 Lombard Street
892-4455
Polish

Schimshacks
2943 Upper Mountain Road
Pekin
731-4111

New York City (212)

Barbetta
321 West 46th Street
246-9171
Italian

The Box Tree
242 East 50th Street
758-8320
French/Continental

Brasserie
100 East 53rd Street
751-4840
Continental

Brazilian Pavilion
141 East 52nd Street
758-8129
Brazilian

Cafe Argenteuil
253 East 52nd Street
753-9273
French

The Chantilly Restaurant
106 East 57th Street
751-2931
French

Chez Pascal
151 East 82nd Street
249-1334
French

Christ Cella's
160 East 46th Street
697-2479
Steaks

The Coach House
110 Waverly Place
777-0303
American

La Cote Basque
5 East 55th Street
688-6525
French

Le Cygne
53 East 54th Street
759-5941
French

Czech Pavilion
313 East 58th Street
752-9199
Continental

Dardanelle's
86 University Place
242-8990
Armenian

David K's Chung Kuo Yuan
1115 Third Avenue
371-9090
Chinese

Dodin-Bouffant
405 East 58th Street
751-2790

Gloucester House
37 East 50th Street
755-7394
Seafood

La Grenouille
3 East 52nd Street
752-1495
French

King Crab
871 Eighth Avenue
765-4393
Seafood

Kitcho
22 West 46th Street
575-8880
Japanese

Le Levandou
134 East 61st Street
838-7987
French

Lutece
249 East 50th Street
752-2225
French

Le Manoir
120 East 56th Street
753-1448
French

Maxwell's Plum
1181 First Avenue
628-2100

Mr. and Mrs. Foster's Place
242 East 81st Street
535-1234

Nanni al Valletto
133 East 61st Street
838-3939
Italian

Orsini's
41 West 56th Street
757-1698
Italian

The Palace
420 East 59th Street
355-5152
French

Palm
837 Second Avenue
687-2953
Seafood and Steaks

Parioli Romanissimo
1466 First Avenue
288-2391
Italian

Pen and Pencil
205 East 45th Street
682-8660
Steak House

Le Perigord Park
575 Park Avenue
752-0050
French

Peter Luger
178 Broadway
Brooklyn
387-7400
Steaks

La Petite Ferme
973 Lexington Avenue
249-3272
French

Le Plasir
969 Lexington Avenue
734-9430
French

Primavera
1570 First Avenue
861-8608
Italian

Quo Vadis
26 East 63rd Street
838-0590
French

Rainbow Room
30 Rockefeller Plaza
757-9090

Restaurant Leslie
18 Cornelia Street
675-1255

La Residence
1568 First Avenue
628-4100
French

Rincon de Espana
226 Thompson Street
475-9891
Spanish

Shun Lee Palace
155 East 55th Street
371-8844
Chinese

Sign of the Dove
1110 Third Avenue
861-8080
French

Tavern on the Green
67th and Central Park West
873-3200
Continental

Trattoria da Alfredo
90 Bank Street
929-4400
Italian

NORTH CAROLINA
Chapel Hill (919)

Restaurant La Residence
220 West Rosemary Street
967-2506
French

NORTH DAKOTA
Mandan (701)

Gourmet House
Interstate 94 and
Memorial Highway
663-9801

OHIO
Cincinnati (513)

Caruso's
610 Main Street
421-1718
Italian

The Celestial Restaurant
Highland Towers
1071 Celestial Street
241-4455

Charley's Crab
9769 Montgomery Road
891-7000
Seafood

Chester's Road House
9678 Montgomery Road
793-8700
American

China Gourmet, Inc.
3340 Erie Avenue
East Hyde Park Village Mall
871-6612
Chinese

La Rosa's Italian Inn
2409 Boudinot Avenue
451-1334
Italian

**The Last National
Bank Restaurant**
105 West Fourth Street
621-1811

Lenhardt's
151 West McMillan
281-3600
German

Magic Wok
8063 Montgomery Road
984-2222
Chinese

Mecklenburg Gardens
302 East University
281-5353
German

New World Food Shop, Inc.
347 Ludlow Avenue
861-1101
Vegetarian

Pigall's
127 West Fourth Street
721-1345
French

Samurai Kabuki Japanese Steak House
126 East Sixth Street
421-1688

Skyline Chili
643 Vine Street
241-2020
Cincinnati Chili

The Sovereign
810 Matson Place
Queens Tower
471-2250
British

Thomas' F&N Steak House
Mary Inglis Highway (Route 8)
261-6766

Cleveland (216)

Balaton Restaurant
12521 Buckeye Road
921-9691
Hungarian

Earth by April
2151 Lee Road
Cleveland Heights
371-1438
Vegetarian

The French Connection
Stouffers
24 Public Square
696-5600
French

Giovanni's
25550 Chagrin Boulevard
Beachwood
831-8625
Italian

Jim Swingos Key and Quarter
1800 Swingos Court
861-5501
Continental

Market Street Exchange
2516 Market Street
579-0520
Continental

The Middle East Restaurant
1012 Prospect Avenue
771-2647
Middle Eastern

Pearl of the Orient
21021 Van Aken Boulevard
Shaker Heights
751-8181

Steffons Gourmet Wizardry
29425 Chagrin Boulevard
Pepper Pike
464-2980
French

The Taverne of Richfield
Front Street Route 176 at
Route 303
Richfield
659-3155

That Place on Bellflower
11401 Bellflower Road
231-4469
Continental

Lakewood (216)

Pier W
12700 Laske Avenue
228-2250
Seafood

OKLAHOMA
Choctaw (405)

Heinz & Crystal's Old Germany Restaurant
29th Street, West of Indian
Meridian Road
390-8647
German

OREGON
Aurora (503)

Aurora Colony Inn
108 Main Street
678-1300
American

Portland (503)

L'Auberge
2180 West Burnside Street
223-3302
French

Bush Garden
900 S.W. Morrison Street
226-7181
Japanese

Couch Street Fish House
105 3rd Avenue N.W.
223-6173
Seafood

Dan and Louis Oyster Bar
208 S.W. Ankeny Street
227-5906

L'Escargot
1987 N.W. Kearney Street
223-6964
French

Genoa
2832 S.E. Belmont Street
238-1464

Nendel's Inn
9900 S.W. Canyon Road
297-2551
American

The Rheinlander
5035 N.E. Sandy Boulevard
288-5503
German

PENNSYLVANIA
Philadelphia (215)

Le Bec-Fin
1312 Spruce Street
732-3000
French

Deja Vu
1609 Pine Street
546-1190
French

The Garden
1617 Spruce Street
546-4455
French

Maureen
11 South 21st Street
567-9895
French

Mitchell's
207 South Juniper Street
735-1299
American

La Panetiere
1602 Locust Street
546-5452
French

Ristorante da Gaetano
727 Walnut Street
922-3771
Italian

Riverfront Restaurant
Delaware Avenue at Poplar Street
925-7000
American

Siva's
34 South Front Street
925-2700
Indian

Pittsburgh (412)

Alex Tambellini's Wood Street
213 Wood Street
281-9956
Seafood

De Foro's
Lawyer's Building
Forbes Avenue
391-8873
Italian/French

Le Mont
1114 Grandview Avenue
431-3100
French

La Normande
5030 Centre Avenue
621-0744
French

Park Schenley
3955 Bigelow Boulevard
Oakland
681-0800
French/Italian

Reading (215)

Joe's
7th and Laurel Street
373-6794
American

RHODE ISLAND
Newport (401)

The Black Pearl
Bannisters Wharf
846-5264
French

SOUTH CAROLINA
Charleston (803)

Roberts of Charleston
42 North Market Street
577-7565

SOUTH DAKOTA
Sioux Falls (605)

The Lafayette
228 North Phillips
332-2383

TENNESSEE
Knoxville (615)

Regas Restaurant
318 North Gay Street N.W.
637-9805

TEXAS
Dallas (214)

Arthur's
1000 Campbell Centre
361-8833
American

Auberge Les Saison
165 Turtle Creek Village
528-1102
French

Calluaud
2619 McKinney
823-5380
French

La Cave
2926 Henderson
826-2190

Chateaubriand
2515 McKinney
741-1223

Chiquita
3810 Congress
521-0721
Mexican

Fuji-Ya
13050 Cort Road
690-8396

Gennies's Bishop Grille
308 North Bishop Avenue
946-1752
Country

Guadalajara
3308 Ross Avenue
823-9340
Mexican

Hunan
5214 Greenville Avenue
369-4578
Chinese

Il Sorrento
8616 Turtle Creek
Boulevard
352-8759
Italian

Jean Claude
2520 Cedar Springs
653-1823
French

Lombardi's
2815 McKinney
823-6040
Italian

Mario's Restaurant
135 Turtle Creek Village
521-1135
Italian

Old Warsaw
2610 Maple Avenue
528-0032
Continental

Pyramid Room
Fairmont Hotel
Ross and Akard Street
748-5454

S&D Oyster Company
2701 McKinney
823-6350
Seafood

Forth Worth (817)

Angelo's
2533 White Settlement Road
332-0357
Barbecue

Cattlemen's
2458 North Main
624-3945
Steak House

Old Swiss House
5412 Camp Bowie
738-8091

Houston (713)

Ché Plaza Hotel
5020 Montrose
524-9071
Seasonal/Continental

**Don's Seafood Restaurant
& Creole Steakhouse**
307 North Belt East
931-7654

Foulard's
10001 Westheimer
789-1661
French

Nanny's
4729 Calhoun
741-7085
Country

Ninfa's
2704 Navigation
228-1175
Mexican

Otto's
5502 Memorial
864-2573
Barbecue

The Rainbow Lodge
1 Birdsall
861-9407

Ruth's Chris Steakhouse
6213 Richmond
782-2453

San Jacinto Inn
San Jacinto Battleground
Off Highway 225
479-2828
Seafood

Zorba the Greek's Café
202 Tuam
528-1382
Greek

San Antonio (512)

Los Arcos Café
5025 Zrzamora
432-9035
Texan and Mexican

**El Bosque Mexican
Restaurant and Patio**
12656 West Avenue
494-2577

Fig Tree Restaurant
515 Villita Street
733 River Walk
224-1976
Continental

**Hung Fong Chinese and
American Restaurant**
3624 Broadway
822-9211

Little Rhein Steak House
La Villita
2315 Alamo
225-2111

La Louisiane
2632 Broadway
225-7984
French

El Micador
722 South St. Mary's
225-9444
Texan and Mexican

Naples
3210 Broadway
826-9554
Italian

Paesamo's
1715 McCullough
226-9541
Italian

UTAH
Salt Lake City (801)

La Caille at Quail Run
9565 South Wasatch Boulevard
942-1751
French

Le Fleur de Lys
338 South State
359-3753
French

The Roof Restaurant
Hotel Utah
Main at South Temple
531-1000
French

The Towne Hall
Salt Lake Hilton
151 West 5th South
532-3344
Seafood

VERMONT
Manchester Depot (802)

Toll Gate Lodge
Routes 11 and 30
362-1779
Continental

VIRGINIA
Great Falls (703)

L'Auberge Chez Francois
332 Springdale Road
759-3800

WASHINGTON
Seattle (206)

Anniques
2037 6th Avenue
624-2296

Canlis'
2575 Aurora Avenue North
283-3313

The Golden Lion
Olympic Hotel
5th and University
682-7700

Ivar's Salmon House
401 N.E. Northlake Way
632-0767
Seafood

Jake O'Shaughnessey's
100 Mercer Street
285-1897
American

Mirabeau
4th and Madison
624-4550
French

Rosellini's Four-10
2512 Fourth Avenue
624-5464
Italian

Rosellini's Other Place
319 Union Street
623-7340

WEST VIRGINIA
White Sulpher Springs (304)

The Greenbrier
536-1110

WISCONSIN
Milwaukee (414)

Anchorage Restaurant
4700 North Port Washington
Road
962-4710

Le Bistro
509 West Wisconsin Avenue
271-7250
French

The English Room
Pfister Hotel
424 East Wisconsin Avenue
273-8222

**Old Town Serbian
Gourmet House**
522 West Lincoln Avenue
672-0206
Serbian

Jean-Paul Restaurant Francais
811 East Wisconsin Avenue
271-5400
French

**Nicolo Ristorante
Internazionale**
1332 East Brady
276-7477
Italian

WYOMING
Jackson Hole (307)

Grand Teton National Park
733-4647
Open Summers Only

Index of Recipes